Roger Crittenden

The Thames and Hudson
Manual of Film Editing

with 67 illustrations

Thames and Hudson

Frontispiece: Griffith was the first major film-maker to demonstrate, by the use of close shots such as this in *Intolerance*, that editing could be a vital part of film-making

© 1981 Thames and Hudson Ltd, London

First published in the USA in 1981 by Thames and Hudson, Inc., 500 Fifth Avenue, New York, New York 10110

Library of Congress Catalog Card Number 81-50796

Printed and bound in Great Britain

THE THAMES AND HUDSON MANUALS

GENERAL EDITOR: W. S. TAYLOR

Film Editing

Contents

Introduction

In 1924 the painter Fernand Léger, fired with enthusiasm for the 'limitless plastic possibilities' of cinema, had this to say about film-makers: 'In spite of their unquestionable talent they are caught between a scenario that must remain a means and the moving image that must be the end. They often confuse the two things. . . . Nevertheless, their means are infinite, unlimited; they have this amazing power to personify, to give a complete life to a fragment. The close-up is their alphabet, they can give plastic identity to a detail. . . . Before this invention you never had the shadow of an idea about the personality of fragments.' (*Bulletin de l'Effort Moderne.*)

It is this 'power to personify, to give a complete life to a fragment', that gives film editing its important function in the craft of the cinema. If these fragments were left unstructured, film would remain an exciting toy. By adding the opportunity to juxtapose and control them, editing completes the cycle of film. Learning to translate the words on paper into effective visual expression is the most important of all lessons. The knowledge of how editing works is the absolute prerequisite of every attempt to make a film.

If a film is to succeed, the writing and direction must already contain the pulse which signifies the way editing can breathe life into the material. To describe the close-up as the film-maker's alphabet is too simple an expression of the basis of film language. Certainly it is important to be aware of the relative values of the various kinds of shot, from long shot to close-up, but to deny the contribution of lighting, camera movement, art direction, performance and the sound track is to exclude most of the armoury at our disposal. From the point of view of the editor it is important to understand how each of these elements contributes to film. Anthony Wollner wrote in *American Cinemeditor* (Spring 1965): 'An editor need not be a writer but he must know story structure; he need not be a cameraman but he must understand pictorial composition and the compatability of angles; he need not be a director, but he must feel the actors' performances and the dramatic or comedy pacing as surely as the director.'

So the contribution of editing to film-making is a two-way process. All the important contributors to a film before it is cut must appreciate the way editing works and the editor must realize how each of the other crafts function to produce the material he works with. It is this mutual understanding that lies at the root of all well-conceived and well-realized films. The director must be in control of the whole process, otherwise the chances are that the cutting room will function merely as a casualty ward applying sticking plaster to the accidents that occurred during shooting.

It is this need to place editing in context that has dictated the structure of this book. Before we confront the process of editing we must look first at the historical development of the language, and then at ways in which various aspects of shooting can help editing to function properly. Then, after having described the cutting room and editing equipment, and the chronological sequence of the process, we examine the language of editing and the way it has been applied by a number of films. The last chapter looks to the future: the choice between film and video.

As you embark on this journey there is one important factor to bear in mind. The opportunities to be vulgar, slick and facetious are manifest in every cutting decision. The temptation to manipulate the material that you are given is not easy to resist. After all, celluloid is divorced from the reality it has captured. We can feel safe with two-dimensional images which do not answer back when we play our tricks with them. Editing is rather like bullfighting: it is all too tempting to go for loud and frequent *olés* from the audience. Even with well-made films the need for discipline and restraint in the editing is an overwhelming responsibility. The editor must be the conscience that protects the director and his audience from indulgence and the reduction of life to the superficial. Even if film functions as an escape for the audience, that escape must be grounded in life-enhancing attitudes.

When you have learned the skills of cutting well enough to make a proper contribution to films you edit, you must still remember that the way you apply those skills will always be more important than the skills themselves. The craft is only a means to an end and not an end in itself.

1 Auguste and Louis Lumière, pioneers of cinematography, whose work suggested ways in which film could structure reality

1　The historical perspective: how the function of editing has evolved

2　Georges Méliès, an early explorer of the magic of film

It is the object of this chapter to point out a few of the crucial developments in the history of film which have impinged on the role that editing plays. No definitive history of this kind has been published in English and all we can do here is to scratch the surface, knowing that our chief objective is to encourage an awareness of some of the factors which have affected the application of the craft of editing. If we were to chart the connections over the last eighty years between developments in film language that have impinged on the function of editing the resulting diagram would be very confusing. Arrows would have to go back and forward in time and sideways across different types of film and individual examples. There has been no single line of progression: indeed, all that can be stated with any degree of conviction is that all cinema can be traced to one of two roots. At the turn of the century the Lumière brothers and Georges Méliès were pioneering the alternate ways that film could develop. The Lumières were demonstrating how events could be the sufficient basis of film reality and Méliès was showing how manipulation of reality could become a film event.

It is a remarkable fact that the basic language of the cinema was established within ten years of the first practical demonstration of projected moving pictures. Although it is common practice to cite the films of D. W. Griffith between 1908 and 1914 as the first to contain the elements which allow us to juxtapose different types of shot when cutting, most of these elements had previously been 'discovered' around the turn of the century by a group of British film-makers. These pioneers (R. W. Paul, Cecil Hepworth, James Williamson, G. A. Smith and Alfred Collins) incorporated close-ups, sequencing of action, parallel action, variation of set-up and camera movement in their films. In *British Creators of Film Technique* (1948) Georges Sadoul suggested that these early film-makers were in fact following principles of sequence and change of view established before cinema in the telling of stories with lantern slides.

THE SILENT ERA

This sequencing with slides can be regarded as the direct antecedent of film editing. But in its early days, film derived its impact from other traditions, including theatre and literature, which might have been expected to dictate completely the way the new medium communicated. However, one important factor made it imperative for film to develop a language that was not dependent upon these other forms: for thirty years (until 1928) film was silent, and title-cards were never a complete substitute for the subleties of story-telling and drama which had been developed over centuries. There was a deadness in images that depended upon the action in each scene usually being shown from one point of view. Without words as a vehicle for complex narrative, adherence to the three unities of Greek tragedy – time, place and action – was always going to inhibit the development of film language. Imitation of the theatre's proscenium view further limited cinema to little more than a series of mute tableaux.

Almost unconsciously, the early film-makers sensed that it was necessary to find ways of controlling rhythm and pace, establishing mood, providing emphasis and focusing attention in the scene. As long as the length of films was restricted to one reel (about 12 minutes) and title-cards could be liberally interspersed, the lazy or uncreative director could get away with one camera position that contained the action of each segment. However, the longer film, containing more than just a series of incidents, was bound to put pressure on this simple form.

THE CONTRIBUTION OF D. W. GRIFFITH

Although other early film-makers had used many of the elements of film language, it was without doubt Griffith's incorporation of such elements into his films which propelled the commercial film forward and gave it a legitimate and coherent form. The techniques used by Griffith – summarized below – are important because they assumed the need for an editing process.

DATE	FILM	TECHNIQUE
1908	*Adventures of Dollie*	Flashback
1908	*For Love of Gold*	Full shot of two characters
1908	*After Many Years*	Close-up of one character and cutback to character being thought of in previous close-up
1909	*The Lonely Villa*	Parallel action
1910	*Ramona*	Extreme long shot
1911	*The Lonedale Operator*	Crosscut close-ups
1912	*The Massacre*	Moving camera, rapid cutting, crosscutting, parallel development and close-up in detail
1914	*Home Sweet Home*	Tracking shot

Iris Barry delineated Griffith's achievements in her monograph, *D. W. Griffith: American Film Master* (1940). Ernest Lindgren spelt them out even more clearly in *The Art of the Film* (1948): 'Griffith instinctively saw the coherence he could achieve on the screen [through editing] even though his material was fragmentary, filmed at different times in different places with a variety of shots but all coming together to make one scene; [Griffith] succeeded in building up in the minds of his audience an association of ideas welded with such logic and charged with such emotional momentum that its truth was not questioned'.

Thus it became apparent that it was possible to make complex choices about each moment and to make those segments cohere. By having the courage and perception to relate his camera position to precisely what he wanted the audience to see at a given moment, Griffith proved that the cinema could develop into a subtle and complex means of expression.

Consider the alternatives open to the film-maker as a consequence of this establishment of the basic language. Let us take as our example the filming of a scene between two people. In 1908 Griffith started out as a director in the knowledge that the conventional film would show the whole scene from beginning to end from a static viewpoint in front of the scene that included the whole area of the action (usually a three-walled set). When he and his cameraman Billy Bitzer decided to move in to a closer shot of one character the convention was broken. When the studio bosses saw the result they complained that this was unacceptable because they had paid for the whole actor! As soon as this closer shot has been seen it is no great step to show a closer shot of the other character. Having done this you can intercut the two. The size of these closer shots can subsequently be varied.

Perhaps the greatest step in this exploration of filmic space is the moment when the director realizes that he is inside the area established in the wide shot. It is as if a member of the audience at a theatrical performance had stepped on to the stage. The camera has to all intents and purposes become a character in the scene. So the dynamics of film language come to depend upon the sense that each member of the audience has of being present in the action through the agency of the camera.

THE CONVENTION

Although this concept goes beyond the general grammar that Griffith incorporated, it is important to acknowledge that it was his opening up of the possibilities that led the way to the establishment of the complete panoply of shots and editing alternatives which we now take for granted. However, we should also be aware of the restrictions that he and others were imposing on the future of conventional cinema at the same time.

Most cinema, ironically, still proceeds as if Griffith were leaning over the shoulder of the director. Each director prepares the shooting script of a film with a very basic assumption in mind: that for each scene there exists an ideal point of view which establishes the position of the camera for the master shot. This ideal position is usually related to the best way of staging the action to allow the focus of the scene to be adequately encompassed. This establishes a plane of action within a two-dimensional frame of reference. Every subsequent shot that is incorporated *must* refer to the axis of this establishing shot. The only ways of changing that axis are by character movement or camera movement. Thus cinema has created its own artificial form.

This development of a convention dependent on the way space is treated is of utmost importance because it provides us with the elements that editing normally uses in manipulating the film material. As we have seen, Griffith was the first to make disparate elements (shots) cohere into convincing sequences. The culmination of his efforts came in two epic films: *Birth of a Nation* (1915) and *Intolerance* (1916). According to Barry: 'The film *Intolerance* is of extreme importance in the history of cinema. It is the end and justification of that whole school of American cinematography based on the terse cutting and disjunctive assembly of lengths of film.'

THE RUSSIAN INFLUENCE

Griffith had an enormous influence on the post-revolution generation of Russian directors. Barry states that it was 'from his example that they derived their characteristic staccato shots, their measured and accurate rhythms and their skill in joining pictorial images together with a view to the emotional overtones of each so that two images in conjuction convey more than the sum of their visual content'.

In 1919, when the Moscow film school was established, Griffith's films were being shown in Russia for the first time – Lenin himself, aware of the immense value of film to the new Bolshevik state, personally arranged the wide distribution of *Intolerance*. However, Lindgren points out that there was a deeper consciousness developing there: 'It was the directors of the Soviet Union who were the first to understand the full significance of this fact [of film truth] and to exploit it; for editing, as the Russians saw, is nothing less than the deliberate guidance of the thoughts and convictions of the spectator.' Lindgren goes on: 'They clearly perceived ... that editing derived its power ... from the fact that a succession of shots involved a complex set of relationships between them, relationships of idea, of duration, of physical movement and of form.'

Among this generation of directors, all of whom had come under the influence of Griffith, were V. I. Pudovkin, Lev Kuleshov, Dziga Vertov and Sergei Eisenstein. Kuleshov's experiments in montage and the writing and practice of Eisenstein and Pudovkin are still witness to their achievements. A close study of their work in print and on film is essential to any self-respecting director or editor.

They began to explore the significance of editing. In his writings, Vertov rejected all of the artifices involved in film-making except editing. According to Pudovkin, Kuleshov believed that film art begins from the moment the director starts to join together the various pieces of film and demonstrated his concept by experiments in the juxtaposition of simple shots. By cutting together the face of a well-known Russian actor, Ivan Mosjoukine, and various other shots, he was able to prove that the meaning of the combined images was a result of their being juxtaposed. Audiences were convinced that the actor was expressing alternately joy, sadness and other emotions in different scenes when in fact Kuleshov had used the same piece of film on each occasion. It was this creative use of fragments that so excited the Russians.

3 D. W. Griffith directing *Intolerance*. One advantage of silent filming was that the director could shout his instructions through a megaphone during the shooting

EISENSTEIN

Thanks to a student, Vladimir Nizhny, we have a record of Eisenstein's approach to the possible alternatives in film style. In his book *Lessons with Eisenstein* (1962) Nizhny gives a detailed and lively account of classes he attended in the 1930s. He describes intense work on the staging of a particular scene which Eisenstein used as a workshop example. It is the killing of the old moneylender by Raskolnikov in Dostoyevsky's *Crime and Punishment*. After exploring many ways of breaking down the scene Eisenstein convinced his students of the feasibility of handling it in one long developing shot. By choreographing his two characters he was able to suggest a way of sustaining the drama through pacing and visual emphasis without resorting to editing.

Eisenstein summarized the work he had done with the class thus: 'It seems to me that the worry that was affecting many of you at the start, that for us to stage everything in one shot would be boring and uninteresting, has proved unjustified. . . . In our work we have managed to fix all the striking and critical moments in a corresponding close view without changing the camera set-up . . . you have been convinced that mise-en-scene contains in itself all the elements concerned with editing break-up into shots.'

Eisenstein then coined the term 'mise-en-shot' to describe the way staging the action carefully can provide all the dramatic emphasis that would conventionally be conveyed by cutting. His object was not to convince his students that the one-shot solution is necessarily *the aim*, but that proper staging of any scene will reveal the details of dramatic development that allow the director to decide how to photograph the

4 Sergei Eisenstein (centre) during the making of *The Strike* (1923)

scene. In this way a better understanding of the evolving dramatic axis will lead to pacing of performance and relating that to shot breakdown.

Traditionally, Eisenstein has been taken to represent the montage approach to filmic construction. This has always been contrasted with the way conventional cinema had used editing as a support to narrative without attempting to convey ideas through specific juxtapositions. Thus the 'Odessa Steps' sequence in *Battleship Potemkin* (1925) uses more than 150 shots in less than 7 minutes to portray an event through complex juxtapositions whereas a film of that incident which aimed merely to convey the surface drama could have been satisfactorily constructed with no more than two dozen cuts. However, the number of cuts per minute is not the real issue: Eisenstein was much more concerned with what is juxtaposed than how often he cut. He saw each decision to cut as an opportunity to convey ideas about the events being portrayed rather than just as a means of pacing and focusing a scene. Pudovkin, who also espoused montage or rapid cutting, where he felt it appropriate, was perfectly happy to concentrate attention on the inherent drama of his material without superimposing intellectual ideas through juxtaposition. Eisenstein believed that his approach to 'intellectual montage' was an infinitely more important creative act.

LIMITATIONS OF THE FORM

Notwithstanding the achievements of Griffith and Eisenstein, for most film-makers in the silent era there were particular restrictions on the mode of representation which dictated the way they structured their material. Firstly, the screen ratio was virtually square (1:1.33). This shape inhibited the inclusion of all significant action within the frame. It was natural therefore to use the cut as a device for emphasis. The lack of sound restricted the methods of conveying subtleties of narrative. The close-up was a natural substitute. The camera was normally static, and its lenses did not have much depth of focus. Again, cutting could overcome this. Performers were either theatrically trained or lacked a sense of the needs of the camera. The cut could compensate for this by either playing down their theatricality or showing the detail that conveyed the desired interpretation of the scene. All or some of these restrictions were occasionally overcome by the best directors, but in normal practice editing was an essential part of compensating for them.

The irony was that the most far-reaching revolution, the coming of sound, at first actually tended to inhibit development. Since it was now possible to convey all essential details of narrative in words, all but the most disciplined and creative directors could depend upon the verbal as a substitute for the visual. This tended to inhibit the imaginative application of editing and to neutralize film style. The tendency continues to this day: most television drama still depends upon people talking to each other, and television documentary substitutes narration for a truly cinematic presentation.

For purely technical teasons, it is not really surprising that initially the response to sound was unimaginative. In its very early days sound-recording technology was extremely primitive. To obtain a usable track, microphones had to be placed very close to the artists and the camera had to remain static. It was difficult to accommodate variations in voice level and the artists could only move if the microphone position was adjustable. Also, early sound recording was virtually non-selective, so acoustics and the control of background sound were crucial.

The result was that most dramatic films in the early 1930s were as artifical and as 'stagey' as silent films had tended to be in the early 1900s. It was left to film-makers who were working in areas other than the dramatic film to point the way to future developments.

ROBERT FLAHERTY AND THE DOCUMENTARY MOVEMENT

One of the most important of these film-makers was the American Robert Flaherty. Known as 'the Father of Documentary' his significance was greater still. As is often true of those who exert a major influence on a new medium, Flaherty had few collaborators, preferring to struggle along his own idiosyncratic path. From *Nanook of the North* (released in 1922) to *Louisiana Story* (1948) Flaherty worked at refining his approach to documentary film in an uncompromising fashion. Although the 'authenticity' of his films has been overstated, there is no doubt that the origins of the continuing debate about the attitudes of the film-maker to his subject and the ethics of how film material should be treated, date back to Flaherty. This is especially true of editing. When we cut a documentary film, our concern to respect the people and events that we manipulate is due in no small part to Flaherty.

Stemming directly from Flaherty but adding its own dimension to the development of film language was the Documentary Movement inspired by John Grierson. Members of this movement were always eager to use editing as a prominent plank in their creative interpretation of reality.

5 Robert Flaherty (centre) during the making of *Louisiana Story*, with (from left to right) Richard Leacock, his cameraman, Helen van Dongen, his editor, the boy in the film and Mrs Flaherty

Music, poetry and visual montage were essential ingredients in the fabrication of their documentary films. They were never concerned with denying the artifice involved though they would have argued that their material and the structure of it still retained the spirit of its 'reality'.

It is a salutary comment on the barrenness of the entertainment film of the 1930s and early 1940s to remember that much of the most exciting and influential work in film was done through public sponsorship in Britain. Grierson masterminded the GPO film unit and through it nurtured a body of talent that culminated both in works of social significance and in the poetic cinema of Humphrey Jennings. By encouraging the involvement of painters, composers and poets, Grierson affirmed that film could develop into a far more significant means of communication than that suggested by mainstream cinema.

CHALLENGING THE CONVENTION

The reaction against the form of the entertainment film was not confined to the documentarists. Another explosion was that set off by the surrealist movement, exemplified by Luis Buñuel's *Un Chien Andalou* (1928) and *L'Age d'Or* (1931). He and others demonstrated that the conjunction of images could rely for coherence on symbolic meaning rather than the linear development of a narrative.

Writing in the late 1940s and 1950s, André Bazin pointed to other explorers who were freeing the cinema from slavish adherence to conventional technique. His heroes from past eras were Flaherty, Friedrich Murnau and Eric von Stroheim and he saw the work of Jean Renoir in the 1930s as continuing the line of realism which he so admired. The central point for Bazin is contained in two quotations from the essays collected in his *Qu'est-ce que le cinéma?* (1959–61): 'When the essence of an event is dependent on the simultaneous presence of two or more factors in the action, *cutting is forbidden*'; and 'The editing of

Kuleshov, of Eisenstein and of Gance didn't show the event: they made an allusion to it'.

It is an oversimplification to consider that Bazin completely disagreed with cutting. His importance lies in the fact that he made us aware that all technique, including editing, has the tendency to intrude between the audience and the film. His effect was to free a whole generation, especially the French directors of the New Wave, from adherence to the neutral style of mainstream cinema. He saw that every intelligent film-maker has an obligation to respect his material and his personal vision, and to use the techniques at his disposal to create a style appropriate to his subject. Bazin's contribution is clearly and cogently analysed by Gavin Millar in *The Technique of Film Editing* (1967).

Both Renoir with *The Rules of the Game* (1939) and Orson Welles with *Citizen Kane* (1941) confirmed for Bazin that it was possible, indeed essential, to treat style as a support to each particular film rather than to accept any preconceived notions of form. The film-maker thus becomes an explorer rather than a presenter. The film should be evidence of the journey not a report of the findings.

CAMERA-STYLO AND CINEMA-VÉRITÉ

Such a release from the shackles of convention was bound to be reflected in subsequent work. Both documentary and fiction exhibited this new-found freedom in the late 1950s and 1960s. Naturally, French film-makers were at the root of much of this development. Alexandre Astruc, a friend of Bazin, coined the term 'Camera-Stylo' (the camera as pen) to describe the way he felt the director should be the direct author of his work.

In the 1960s the Cinema-Vérité movement attempted in documentary to use the dynamic of real events with a minimum of editing manipulation. 16 mm lightweight cameras and recorders made it possible to film in actual situations *without* the camera dictating how events were shown. It was felt that film had by and large, and quite wrongly, become slave to the camera. However, in practice the films of Chris Marker and Jean Rouch in France and Richard Leacock and others in America, for instance, did not reduce editing to the minimal function of joining bits of 'reality' together that seems to be implied by this approach.

Unless it is envisaged that there is no limit to the final length of the film certain compromises have to be reached either about what to shoot and/or what to cut. Several solutions were found by the proponents of Cinema-Vérité. One was to start with a question. Thus Rouch and Edgar Morin decided in *Chronique d'un Eté* (1961) to build the film around asking people in Paris if they were happy. By using this specific question they were able to structure the film around responses and the way the responses suggested further material to be filmed. Thus the film had a quasi-organic development, even though Rouch and Morin were not above contriving meetings and encounters that seemed to grow out of material already obtained. Another 'compromise' developed by the movement was to structure films around a coherent event: the reality to be filmed provided the basis for the film's structure even before the cameras started turning. This was especially true of the Drew-Leacock-Pennebaker films: *Primary* (1960), *Football* (1961), *The Chair* (1962) and

6 A still from *Chronique d'un Eté*, a film in which Jean Rouch and Edgar Morin consciously explored documentary style and technique

Jane (1963) are all good examples of subjects that rely on the dynamic contained in the situation being filmed for the basis of their central structure. Perhaps the most important logical conclusion to be reached from this style of film-making is that there is every reason for director and cameraman (and editor) to be the same person. This was exactly the conclusion reached by Albert Maysles after shooting for Godard on the latter's segment of *Paris vue par . . .* (1963).

THE NEW WAVE

Godard was one of the directors who came to be known as le Nouvelle Vague (the New Wave). What these directors shared was a desire to release film-making from the inhibitions that had been built into it by the pressure of commercial and industrial modes of production. The Italian Neo-Realists had opened up the options by rejecting the artificiality of studio production, and the New Wave directors were further encouraged by Cinema-Vérité, whose documentary film-makers had taken to the streets with minimal equipment and no obligations except to their own ideas and predilections.

The result, in the work of Claude Chabrol, Godard, Alain Resnais and François Truffaut, amongst others, was a new questioning of the language and structuring of narrative film. Most of them had worked on the magazine *Cahiers du Cinéma*, edited by Bazin in its early days, and had been constant visitors to the Paris Cinémathèque where Henri Langlois nurtured their interests and enthusiasm. So not only were they soaked in movies, but they had also learned at the master's knee the need for a coherent and consistent approach to their craft. Their particular styles and approaches to cinema were too divergent to have stemmed directly from Bazin's precepts in their particular approaches to cinema. However, their attitudes to editing had certain things in common. Much of their work demonstrates a refreshing openness that defies the rules and throws over a slavish adherence to the convention. By having the language at their fingertips they were able to use its grammar in a dynamic way rather than reproducing a sterile form.

To take one example: the dissolve had become the device for conveying the passage of time. Truffaut amongst others questioned both the need to use the dissolve in this way and even the need to signal time passing so conventionally. This released the device to other uses, especially to convey emotional connections between the content of images. It also allowed the simple cut to exist as a transitional device, controlling the rhythm of the juxtaposed shots in such a way that the dissolve became redundant.

The New Wave achieved a great deal more by questioning the basic language of cinema. Until the 1960s, dramatic film had assumed that every scene had to contain narrative development. It seems simple now to ask why such weight should be applied to every cut. But just as simply the answer then was that there was no inherent reason except that the convention demanded it. Once released from this prime function editing can be used to do much more. Suddenly traditional drama seems an unnecessarily restrictive means of expression. We have at our disposal a medium which, while continuing to tell stories, can also concentrate on states of mind and the exploration of relationships that are not dependent upon conventional narrative development. Out of this freedom came Michelangelo Antonioni's *L' Avventura* (1959) which is based on no more story than a dilatory search for a missing woman but which, within that slight framework, is actually concerned with portraying the empty lives of a group of upper-class Italians. Godard used some elements of the thriller genre in *Pierrot le Fou* (1965) to explore attitudes to surface reality and some of the influences on our life in capitalist society. Truffaut used a triangle of relationships in *Jules et Jim* (1961) where the events are dependent on nothing more substantial than the whims of the heroine Catherine.

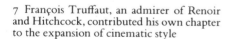

7 François Truffaut, an admirer of Renoir and Hitchcock, contributed his own chapter to the expansion of cinematic style

EXPLORING THE BOUNDARIES

To some extent Resnais's exploration of time and memory, especially in
L'Année Dernière à Marienbad (1961), represents the extreme of this new-
found freedom. We do not have to like his film to realize that it is
important to understand the driving force behind such an approach: a
desire to use cinema for more than straightforward story-telling. Resnais
is far more interested in aspects of our mental life and sees cinema as
capable of demonstrating the way our thought processes layer reactions
to the real world in a constantly evolving way. He has confronted the
basic linear nature of film and demands that we too become aware that
past, present and future are not blocked off from each other.

Resnais's films are not popular. The demands they make of the viewer
make it predictable that the mass audience will always reject them. This
does not make his films irrelevant. The exploration of any medium will
always be reflected in the development of the mainstream in the future.
As far as editing is concerned, the ebb and flow of style can be predicted
to progress gingerly towards the inclusion of more subtle and
sophisticated techniques. Since the New Wave, individual directors
working in the commercial cinema have incorporated elements that
seemed avant-garde in the 1960s. Others have continued to explore
avenues of their own.

Robert Bresson, for instance, has pursued an ascetic and pure style that
eschews much still espoused by conventional film. The Hungarian
Miklos Jancso has taken the mise-en-shot principle to the extreme of 8-
minute takes, choreographing camera and performers to substitute for
the cut. Meanwhile, in some observational documentary, especially
ethnographic, uninterrupted filming of events has kept faith with Bazin's
precept.

COLOUR AND WIDE SCREEN

Whereas the silent film was black-and-white with only a few experiments
in colour, by the 1930s the full spectrum was available to the film-maker
and economically viable. These days it is very rare for black-and-white
to be used. Notable exceptions such as Peter Bogdanovitch's *Last Picture
Show* (1971) and Woody Allen's *Manhattan* (1979) have resurrected the
glories of black-and-white. For a long time, however, people such as
Bergman and Kurosawa preferred monochrome photography and only
commercial pressures finally made the possibility of choice a faint one.
However, now that colour stock is proving unstable a revival of black-
and-white is likely.

Colour holds particular dangers for the film-maker, which can become
all too apparent in the editing room. The temptation to be merely
colourful leads to cluttered art direction and less discipline with regard
to composition and choice of shot. For Luchino Visconti in say *Death in
Venice* (1970) this led to a shooting style which made every shot a tour
de force but seems to have created problems in sequencing. On many
occasions the cut was an interruption rather than an aid to providing the
necessary flow. In the right hands, consciousness of the advantages of
black-and-white can lead to an interesting marriage. This was true in
Michael Powell's *A Matter of Life and Death* (1946) where the scenes in

'heaven' were rendered in black-and-white while those on earth were shot in colour. In both contexts the art direction was carefully controlled to support this choice.

Wide screen had also been experimented with in the silent era. Abel Gance's *Napoleon* (1925) employed an incredible technique which sometimes appeared on the screen as a triptych. Commercially it was the advent of Cinemascope in 1953 with *The Robe* that made alternative aspect ratios a reality. The effect of wide screen on cutting technique is well analysed by Millar in *The Technique of Film Editing*. In the hands of a master such as Elia Kazan – *Wild River* (1960), *East of Eden* (1955), *The Arrangement* (1969), etc. – it is a revelation, but for many the effect on composition and the control of movement within the frame is all too intimidating. For wide screen can exacerbate the need for consciousness of the focus of interest in the frame. In continuity cutting the junction between two images should take advantage of the audience's expectation of both the relations of the new shot to the preceeding one, and more importantly the area of the frame that is to be concentrated on. If, for instance, the cut is taking advantage of a movement that is continued across the cut it is ineffective to show a medium shot of someone walking which cuts to a wide high angle where the person is an insignificant detail in the top righthand corner. By the time the audience 'finds' the focus of interest the value of movement as a bridging device is lost. It is interesting that both Eisenstein's mise-en-shot principle and Bazin's preference for continuous action can both be adhered to more easily in wide screen.

TECHNIQUE AND MANIPULATION

In recent years it has become common to hear two opposed views about the best use of editing. On the one hand, it is maintained that the best cutting is invisible, that a seamless smooth construction or a denial of the art by making it invisible should be the aim. On the other, it is suggested that all editing technique should be apparent, that if you are manipulating reality it is more honest to show that you are doing so. The two schools of thought might be assumed to apply to fiction and documentary respectively, but this is not so. Dramatic film often makes good use of allowing the audience to become aware of editing techniques. For instance, both Godard and Rohmer in different ways resist the audience's expectations of a cut. Conversely, many a documentary depends for its credibility on seamless construction.

Attitudes to editing must never be reduced to the opportunist or merely imitative. This chapter has only allowed the barest hint at the complexity of the historical development of the craft, but should prevent the beginner from an approach to editing that ignores the perspective of the past, and should allow you to approach the practical aspects with a due sense of humility and awareness. No cut is made in isolation from the development of cinema thus far, and you ignore at your peril the questions raised by each major contributor to film. The techniques employed by a number of contemporary directors are analysed in Chapter 5.

8, 9 Two masters, Jean Renoir and Luis Buñuel, brought very different conceptions to the same original material in their versions of *Le Journal d'une Femme de Chambre*

2   Shooting with cutting in mind

CREATING THE EDITOR'S MATERIAL

It is essential to be aware from the start of the effect of different styles on the same material. There are many examples available to us from the history of cinema of different directors tackling similar stories. A classic example is how Renoir (in 1945) and Buñuel (in 1964) treated *Le Journal d'une Femme de Chambre*. Had the two versions been given different titles, it would be some time before one became aware of the films having much in common. The translation of Akira Kurosawa's *Rashomon* (1950) into *The Outrage* (1964) by Martin Ritt and of *The Seven Samurai* (1954) into *The Magnificent Seven* (1961) by John Sturges, though not meant to be imitations, are other examples. The various adaptions of Raymond Chandler from Edward Dymytryk's *Farewell My Lovely* (1944) to Robert Altman's *The Long Goodbye* (1972) show the breadth of interpretation available to directors ostensibly working in the same convention.

It is also important to realize the contribution made by cameramen. Henri Decae and Raoul Coutard in a sense created as much of the style of the New Wave as the directors whose approach spawned the so-called

10 Akira Kurosawa directing *The Seven Samurai*. He was influenced by directors such as Ford and subsequently plagiarized by other Western directors

auteur concept. The cameraman is indeed the final proof, if any were needed, of the importance of style. A Hollywood veteran, James Wong Howe, worked with many directors, some brilliant, some competent and some downright mediocre. No matter for whom he was working, he invariably managed to put his own stamp on the imagery that ended up on the screen. It must have been a real pleasure to cut his material together. Examples of close collaboration between cameraman and director are the work done by Walter Lassally for Michael Cacoyannis, especially in black-and-white on such films as *Stella* (1954), *A Girl in Black* (1955) and *A Matter of Dignity* (1957) and that of Sven Nykvist for Ingmar Bergman on numerous films. It is impossible to separate the contributions made by these partners to the finished films. There are also many examples of very good cameramen working with not untalented directors producing material that is disappointing to both. The 'chemistry' is obviously very important: if partnerships are unsuccessful the results will be irredeemable in the cutting room.

So style is not, definitely not, something to be applied in the cutting room. The true function of editing must be to respect the approach predetermined by choices made at earlier stages. If there is nothing to respect there is nothing to contribute, and all the wizardry available to the editor will be to no avail.

CONVENTIONAL COVER AND THE ALTERNATIVES

For the best results, the following questions which affect the editing should be kept in mind during the shooting:

1 Where at any time is the focus of interest?
2 When and to what does that focus shift?
3 What is the mood and therefore consequent pace of the scene? Does that pace change?
4 Are there natural pauses which should be reflected in stillness and silence?
5 What significant detail *must* be seen?
6 Conversely, when is it important to see the whole area in which the action takes place?
7 Is there movement which requires covering?
8 When is a reaction more significant than an action?
9 Does any sound off-screen affect the understanding of the scene?
10 How do the beginning and the end of the scene relate to those immediately before and after?
11 What is the function of the scene in the overall script?

Because these questions are often not easy to answer, the soft option of 'conventional cover' is frequently resorted to. Cover consists of a master shot – wide enough to encompass the whole action; medium shots – usually isolating significant interaction; and close-ups – for emphasis and reaction. In this way cover can be composed of a dozen shots all running the total length or most of the length of a scene.

However, if the above questions are answered in advance two tremendous benefits will be obtained. Firstly, the ratio of shot material to edited footage will be substantially reduced, and secondly – and more importantly in my opinion – the director will have chosen a positive style, avoiding the dreadful neutrality in relation to subject material that is seen in the hack work every day of the week on television screens around the world. Of course, the camera is not the only contributor to this committed point of view. Casting, performance, art direction, choice of locations and many other elements need the same rigorous appraisal in relation to these questions.

Remember, however, that the best scenarios will already contain implicit answers to the questions posed above. The perceptive director will be able to extract the essence and match the original conception with an appropriate style. Bresson has said: 'Build your film on white, on silence and on stillness.' (*Notes on Cinematography*, 1977.) The spare imagery, uncluttered sound track, and static camera in his own films accurately mirror this attitude.

CONTROLLING IMAGE AND SOUND

I discuss the importance of sound in editing in detail in Chapter 6. But it is essential at this early stage to understand the basic interdependence of image and sound. All the best in cinema must give the impression that everything *seen* and *heard* was part of the intention of the film-maker, except in those films which deliberately set out to allow chance and improvisation to play an important part. Superficially, the difference is analogous to that between Mozart and modern jazz (though Mozart in concerti frequently allowed for improvised passages and some modern jazz is scored down to the last note).

According to Bresson, 'the sound track created silence'. Indeed, some years ago a long-playing record, marketed cleverly as the ideal accompaniment to a quiet evening at home, sold like hot cakes even though neither side emitted an audible sound. It had no secondhand value of course as the slightest click put the lie to the label: 'Silence – 25 minutes'. Joseph Losey, asked during a television interview some years ago why he continued to make films against the odds, replied that he was fascinated by the rhythm of silence. The interviewer obviously thought that Losey was being clever and ignored the reply. But if I were asked to write a book on film as a language, I would plagiarize Losey, and call it 'The Rhythms of Silence'. It is imperative to understand at the stage of shooting a film that cutting is not about filling the silence, overriding the stillness or camouflaging the whiteness; as Dr Johnson, in his definition of a net, emphasized, the holes are more important than the material which surrounds them. To take the most obvious example: if two people are talking, there should always be as much significance in the gaps in their conversation as in the words they speak; the space (whiteness) between them should be as interesting as what fills it and their lack of movement as riveting as any action imaginable.

In a scene in Francis Ford Coppola's *The Conversation* (1974), Gene Hackman visits his old girlfriend played by Teri Garr. There is a tension between them, obviously born of his too infrequent visits and the fact that he is secretive about his work as a private investigator. At the point where one feels he wants to convey to her that he may not be calling again, he wanders into the kitchenette, and the silence, distance and stillness are broken by the line: 'Your rent is due this week.' As Bresson also said: 'Don't run after poetry. It penetrates unaided through the joins.'

If by now you are beginning to get the idea that editing a well-shot film ought to be a matter of following a well-signposted route, I am achieving my objective. We must now look at some fairly mechanical ground rules and procedures.

IDENTIFICATION

The clapperboard or slate is the aid to synchronization, filmed at the beginning or end of each take. The 'clapping' of the hinged section provides an exact visual and aural reference point. It also gives slate and take numbers. It presumably originated *c*. 1929–30 when everything, including the inclination of the actors' and actresses' heads (see *Singing in the Rain*, 1952), became slave to the new sound film. It is a remarkably crude device which does nothing to improve the neurotic circumstances pervading the process of shooting a film. There are substitute devices for providing a sync reference and for indicating some kind of numerical sequence, but nothing fulfils the task of identification quite as well as the clapper. Used properly the procedure when clapping is something like the following:

PERSON	VERBAL INSTRUCTION	MECHANICAL OPERATION
Assistant director/director	Quiet	Clapper in shot
Asst. dir./dir.	Run sound	Switch on recorder
Sound recordist	Running/Speed	
Asst.dir./dir.	Run camera	Switch on camera
Camera operator	Running/Speed	
Asst. dir./dir.	Mark it	
Camera asst.	Slate 5 – 3	Clap and exit frame
Director	Action!	

In the shooting of fiction film by American crews, the slate number corresponds to the shot as numbered in the script. This means that there is an instant reference when cutting without having to correlate two sets of numbers. Of course, as soon as you allow flexibility during shooting and begin to add shots not scripted, the numbering system can become complicated.

I have long thought that directors should encourage their actors and actresses not to treat the word 'Action!' as if it were letting greyhounds out of their traps. It is in fact entirely the wrong word as a cue to begin 'acting'. In a theatrical rehearsal the director says 'In your own time' or 'When you're ready'. The best performers will, in any case, set off at the pace and rhythm that best suits the scene, but those less experienced or nervous will hit the end of 'Action!' with their first line, as if they have just received the blast from a twelve bore shot-gun.

This can have a radical effect on the edited film for two reasons. Firstly, pace and rhythm often vary enormously in pieces of speech and movement that have to be dovetailed together; so it is essential that the mechanics of shooting do not dictate that pace and rhythm. Secondly, the existence of a pause after 'Action!' allows the editor a useful second or

PROD. NO.
TITLE
DIRECTOR

| camera no. | roll no. |
| SCENE | TAKE |

11 The clapperboard

two of extra sound overlap and static visual. The best way of achieving these objectives is probably the taking of two or three deep breaths before beginning the 'Action!' The same criteria apply to the end of each shot. The director, camera operator and cast should complete the action and then pause before the director shouts 'Cut!'

In any case, at the beginning and end of every shot, both action and dialogue should extend beyond that part of the script for which the shot is intended. For instance, if someone has just sat down on a chair in the previous shot and you have moved in closer for the dialogue, always repeat the sit-down action. A cut at the point where an action has just been completed is the most uncomfortable of all. In this example it would be as well for the first few lines of dialogue to have been given on the end of the wider shot too.

Sometimes it proves impossible to put a clap on the beginning of a shot; interestingly enough this may be because the director has carefully established the mood for a shot and wants as little as possible to interrupt the performer's concentration. It happens most often in documentaries when the film-maker has no control of a situation and simply hopes to switch on in time for the start of interesting dialogue or action. In these cases an end-board or slate can be used. So, before saying 'Cut!', the director says 'End-board' and the clapper is inserted *upside down*.

For the clapperboard to be used efficiently, the following points should be remembered. The whole process should not normally take more than a few seconds:

1 The board must be chalked up clearly and accurately.
2 The verbal identification should precede the clap and in any case not be simultaneous with it.
3 If a second clap is needed add 'second clap' to verbal identification.
4 The board must be in focus.
5 The board must be big enough in frame to be readable.
6 If lighting or exposure is low you may need to open up the lens or spotlight the board.
7 If the shot is too close to include the whole board, show area of identification for verbal cue and move down for clap.
8 Start with hinged section raised and clap crisply.

9   Hold the board closed and steady for a moment after clap.

10   Leave shot quietly and quickly – have your escape route planned.

When a clapperboard is unavailable or inconvenient, possible alternatives include clapping the hands together horizontally or tapping the head of a microphone with a finger. In documentary shooting with a two-person crew and long takes, you can avoid interrupting the flow with an 'alien' voice by using one of these two methods and showing an increasing number of fingers to the camera for every shot. If a two-person crew is well co-ordinated this can be an efficient identification system. Obviously a visual indication of the slate number is always a useful bonus, so carry a notebook and felt-tip pen with you in case. Even so-called 'blip' sync (where the film is fogged and a high-pitched bleep is recorded on to the tape) works better with the addition of a visible and audible indication of sequential numbering.

RELATING SHOOTING TO EDITING

There are no absolute rules about relating the way a film is shot to problems of cutting. Even the guidelines below can sometimes be ignored to good effect. If, like Godard, your objective is to remind the audience that they are watching a cinematic representation of 'reality', then breaking the convention is part of your stock in trade. Most of the guidelines that follow aim to assist the objective of suspending disbelief in your audience in the face of working in a two-dimensional medium that establishes its own language.

Continuity
All aspects of continuity have very wide implications for the editor. It is no accident that the function of watching continuity has long been established as an important and specific task. Traditionally assigned to a 'continuity girl', this job is a necessary protection for the director in controlling all aspects of staging a scene. It is well known that the consistency of appearance, clothing, props, make-up and so on of actors is the concern of this job, but the best continuity persons will do much more. Lighting, details of design and setting, matching shots and action, provision of cover, consistency of dialogue, indeed everything to ensure that all available shots are indeed usable by the editor, should be the responsibility of this person. Inconsistencies that find their way on to the film must be noted on the continuity sheets as must the reasons for preferred takes and why others are faulty.

The line   This is the mother of all cinematic conventions. Every camera position establishes a plane and consequently everything retains a left-to-right relationship. Once a line is established your alternative camera positions lie within a 180° arc. So, in ill. 12a, if you use positions in the arc B–C you cannot use positions in the arc D–E. Avoiding crossing the line seems to give the inexperienced film-maker his worst problems. And it is extremely frustrating in the cutting room to be presented with shots which, although valid in themselves, cannot be intercut with the rest of the shots for that sequence. It is possible to establish a new line, but this can only be done by moving the camera across the line *during* the shot,

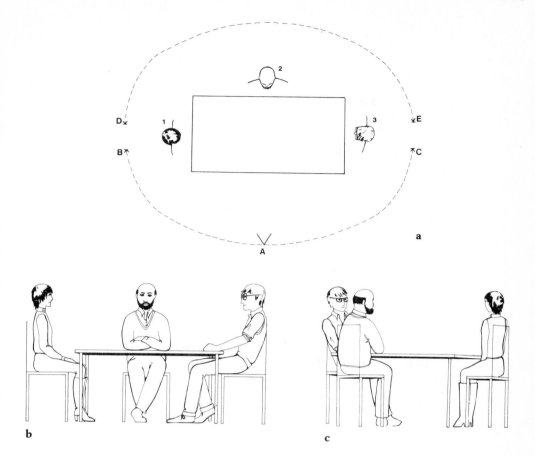

12 The line: if the master shot (*b*) is taken from camera position A (see *a*) only shots within the arc from B to C are possible. Shots in the arc D to E (e.g. *c*) would disorientate the audience because the characters would seem to have changed their relative positions in relation to left and right of the screen

or by the subject crossing the line during the shot. An analysis of most good dramatic films will reveal the positive use of moving to a new line for dramatic emphasis – an effect akin to that experienced in reality when someone moves their position in relation to us sufficiently to require us to decide either to accept or resist the need to turn round in order to face them again. Antonioni is particularly fond of using realignment of this sort to mark psychological shifts in a scene.

Eyelines This is closely related to the problem of line. A simple shot of two or more characters establishes the 'eyelines' or direction of look between them. These physical relationships must be maintained in every shot for the same scene. In essence this means respecting the line that is established by the camera position. It is wrong to assume that if a close-up of one character is being taken from exactly in front, the eyeline principle need not concern you. Looking straight at camera will only be appropriate if it is known that the person being looked at is placed square

 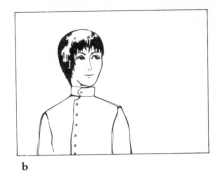

a   b

13 Eyelines: given the same master shot A (see *12b*), all shots of the individual characters must exhibit matching eyelines. For example, in a close-up, character 2 must look screen left at character 1 (*a*), and character 1 must look screen right at both 2 and 3 (*b*)

on to the subject of the shot. As with line, movement of the camera or the subject during a shot can vary the eyeline – and again, dramatic emphasis can be gained, once the eyelines have been established, by a character looking 'the wrong way'.

Direction of movement   Consistency is needed both within the frame and in and out of it. Most simply, if a person or object exits right of frame, they should enter left and vice versa. All movement should retain that continuity. There is one exception: if a character exits frame towards the camera and we wish to cut to a reverse angle of the character seen from behind, he must be seen to re-enter the frame from the same side. This is because the character's movement has broken the line and the reverse angle is on a new line.

Pace of movement   This is much more difficult to remember to match. We have all seen the Western where the posse is riding hell-for-leather in a wide panning shot, and on the cut to a medium head-on tracking shot it seems to have slowed to a sedate trot. All movement needs matching both to be convincing and to allow flexibility in cutting. Walking shots seem to be the hardest movement to match, and it is easy to delude yourself into believing that if the legs are not visible the pace does not matter. But with any action that is going to be cut on, even the turn of a head or the flick of a finger, the pace must be matched in shooting. One of the most obvious mismatches is the cut from the exterior to the interior of a moving vehicle. In this and other cases, the problem often stems from the difficulty encountered by the camera operator in filming close movement. It is best, if possible, to shoot the awkward close shot first and to match the speed that has been achieved when covering the same action wider. There is a similar problem with sound: actors often raise the volume and increase the speed of dialogue when being shot in close-up. I can only surmise that this phenomenon is a reaction to a feeling of intimidation at the proximity of the camera. It can have an alarming effect on the usefulness of cover in a sequence. Strangely enough, it can also be an indication that the scene is best handled wider and the close-ups rejected.

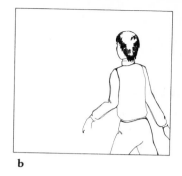

a   b   c

14 Reverse angles: for action where the camera reverses its position to follow a character who has been seen to exit *towards* camera (*a*) the character must re-enter on the same side (*b*). The two camera positions and the movement of the character (indicated by the arrow) are shown in *c*

Angle and distance   Unless there is reason to go for a shock effect or to emphasize the significance of a person or object, it is usually important to vary angle as well as distance in alternative shots. Kurosawa is fond of cutting in on the same camera angle for effect, for example at the dramatic climax of *Sanjuro* (1962) and as the villagers approach the water-mill in *The Seven Samurai*. However, in normal cutting, continuity has to be matched so carefully and the position of the subject in the frame is so critical that it is safest to move at least 30° from the line of other shots for your alternative, especially if the shot is of a single person. The zoom lens has tended to make directors lazy as it enables the size of the subject in the frame to be changed without the camera being moved. A slow zoom-in on the focus of attention in a frame, either static or moving, can of course be very effective, but the temptation to use the beginning and end of the zoom as separate shots should normally be avoided.

Set discipline   There is a very particular discipline needed when shooting on a set or in circumstances which allow you to position the camera to gain a wider perspective than is realistic in a confined space. On location in a room where the windows and doors are impracticable as extensions to the shooting area, all shooting must be contained within the space. The problem in the studio where walls can be 'floated' is that your audience easily loses belief in the artifice presented to them. I have been given rushes where a character is seated on a sofa against one wall of a room and found I had to use as the reverse angle a shot obviously taken from six feet behind the sofa! Wide-angle lenses, used to contain all the action in a confined space, can also give a false impression.

The overlap   I mentioned the value of overlap action when describing the procedure for identification of slates (see p. 27). The important thing when including the cover provided by overlaps is not to assume that cutting on action is essential or even preferable. Indeed, it is often more dramatically effective to cut during a pause that precedes or follows action, otherwise the physical movement in itself may be seen as the most significant factor when in actual fact it is usually the psychological effect of the physical act that needs emphasis. So the overlap should be several seconds *either side* of an action to allow for cutting pre-action, during action and post-action. Of course, if you are certain of the point to cut it is only necessary to include enough overlap to allow the actors to match the 'pitch' of their performance.

Whatever you do, it is imperative not to think that solving the problems of 'conventional cover' is a protection against failure or, worse, a guarantee of success. The mediocre film often demonstrates a foolhardy belief that efficient application of the mechanics of shooting is a substitute for having a clear conception of what you want to show and how to show it. It is also true that an unconventional shooting method still has to find answers to the above problems. The film that is shot in long takes must confront the questions of rhythm and pace, focus of interest and the other factors affecting the use of the camera; and some substitute will have to be found for the language of individual close-ups, medium shots and long shots. Jancso choreographs the camera with a precision exceeding that demanded by the convention. Conversely, R. W. Fassbinder leaves the camera as a passive spectator, albeit in a carefully chosen position, while the action – or inaction – unfolds before it.

DOCUMENTARY SHOOTING

It is also not politic to ignore the requirements of the cutting room when shooting in a less controlled style. Reference to the conventional answers may be irrelevant as interruptions to the 'flow' of such camera work will probably only work if the dramatic 'flow' is conducive to it. The cameraman therefore needs to be all but director and to react to the action with an awareness of the drama unfolding before him.

Uncontrolled shooting obviously places an enormous burden on the editing process. It could be argued that the burden is too heavy and that it is an illustration of the dangers of leaving the editorial decisions to the cutting room. Maybe complete pictorial records, say of tribal rituals, should be stored as reference material for anthropologists or other experts, while the précis that becomes a film is made more generally available. The problem still remains that the demands of film and record are essentially irreconcilable, since the very need for a film language springs initially from setting a limit to the length of time we demand an audience's attention. Andy Warhol sees no need for compromise and therefore no such need for the artifice of cinematic language.

The trend to less preconceived shooting has encouraged the idea of the director/cameraman spontaneously gathering material with an eye and ear to the needs of the cutting room where he or she may well be the best editor of the footage. There is an almost complete duplication of the editing requirements that exist for fiction films: the line, eyelines, direction of movement, change of angle, matching the pace of action, even overlaps. The trouble with the last is that, unless you wish to 'construct' or 'direct' your documentary footage, it is a questionable practice to contrive circumstances where overlaps are available to you. Of course, if interviews are part of the material, a request to the interviewee to start again a little before the end of the statement on the previous take is possible, and the filming of processes or any form of mechanical progression can be covered in the conventional way.

It is of the utmost importance in documentary to try and predict significant action so as to begin filming early and, just as importantly, not to switch off too close to the end of such action. This will allow your material to retain a flexibility in editing that reflects the feel of actual events through the natural variations in rhythm and pace. There is nothing more irritating than to find that an important shot of, say, a train passing through a station, starts with the train already approaching the platform and ends before it has disappeared round the next bend in the track. It is highly likely that the dramatic significance of the shot may lie either in the arrival or departure of the train, not in its mere progression along the platform. It is consciousness of the precise significance that allows the cameraman to cover the essential action. In fiction films action is covered in a similar way, but in documentary the moment of decision is often delayed until it is actually happening before the lens.

One essential difference between much documentary and dramatic films arises from the desire of the documentary film-maker to allow his audience to verify the events he is covering. An aspect of this was noted by Dai Vaughan during the cutting of Granada TV's *Some Women of Marrakesh* (1977), which was directed by Melissa Llewellyn-Davies. He pointed out that the use of complementary angles to *imply* spatial proximity between characters, often of course already established in a wide shot, is a technique not available to the documentary film-maker who is concerned to retain the 'truth' of the events being filmed. However, it is now common practice to include the swing of the camera from one character to another to substitute for complementary angles because it strengthens the feelings of spatial proximity whilst retaining dramatic coherence. The conventional cutaway (e.g. cutting to a shot of another character listening) has lost credibility, except in news coverage, although that is arguably the last category in which events should be knowingly misrepresented. The trouble with the cutaway concept is that it is more often than not used to disguise considerable editing without acknowledging the process.

There is a sense in which the documentary, as conventionally purveyed by television, has not broken loose from the journalistic attitude which says that it is not the subject in itself that is interesting but the way *I* the journalist present it to you – including what *I* choose to include and therefore exclude. This idea of predigesting current affairs has a simple rationale in journalism but should never have been applied so widely to film. It has meant that documentary style has been based on the wrong criteria. You still see sequences in the News where the only way the material could have been obtained was for the action to have been repeated several times so that it could be cut for continuity like a dramatic film. Apart from the waste of time and effort, the method destroys the credibility of the 'story'. It also leads to the ridiculous situation where the News can be the most contrived piece of filming on television.

Documentary then should never be reduced to a script in the sense that drama usually is. The way material is obtained should always be related to the subject of the film and not to an arbitrary set of criteria which give the film-maker a sort of shopping list. Although the same set of questions need to be answered as for dramatic film, where there is a tension between getting the best material and satisfying the ideal requirements for editing, the former must be given preferential treatment.

The following points about documentary shooting will ensure fewer problems in the cutting room:

1   The value of identification and sync reference was discussed in detail on p. 26. There are situations in documentary shooting in which neither is possible but it is better to get into the habit rather than be casual about it. It also ensures better co-ordination between camera and sound since most forms of sync reference require a conscious effort from both. This can prove crucial where material is only useful if picture and sound are obtained in sync. It can be totally frustrating in the cutting room to find, for instance, that the camera pans off a subject too soon or that the recordist switches on too late. End slates are often less intrusive.

2   Where possible allow a static hold at the beginning and end of movement, either of the camera or of the subject of the shot. Pans, tilts, tracking, zooms and hand-held movement are always much easier to cut if there is a static hold at the start and finish of significant action. Of course, even the decision of the cameraman when to pause in this fashion is a stylized reaction to the events being filmed and it is sometimes all too obvious that boredom or tiredness rather than consciousness of the right psychological moment is the deciding factor.

3   Make as much of the shot footage usable as is humanly possible. There is a school of thought amongst documentary cameramen that moments of 'dodgy' shooting should be deliberately sabotaged to avoid the possibility of the errant editor using such sections. This is a very negative attitude and, as every experienced cameraman knows, unless you actually switch off, the editor is likely to use the bit in question anyway. The most crucial decision is always related to the need to refocus. Whereas the feature cameraman has an assistant to control focus and the opportunity to rehearse all movement requiring alterations in focus, such luxury is often not available with documentaries. The technique of adjusting focus while accomplishing any change of shot is not easy, even when both hands are free to operate rather than hold the camera, and precious seconds spent in focusing may provoke the necessity for a cut where continuous action would have been much more desirable. Panning from one character to another should be carefully achieved, even if the first inclination is to get to the new subject as quickly as possible. However, if the circumstances dictate that the shock effect of some event should be seen and the atmosphere is violent or disturbed, a whip-pan may be exactly complementary to the mood of the scene and should then be used.

4   It is sometimes, wrongly, thought that to consider the requirements of continuity when shooting documentaries is to interfere with the reality being filmed. Continuity is, of course, more of a problem to deal with in documentary than in fiction, because the director may not have as much control over his material. However, it must never be ignored. The line and eyeline do not cease to exist because events are 'real'. If, in the middle of an interview, one is presented with material where the participants are seen looking the opposite way to the rest of the scene, it will be unusable unless the change of camera position happens on screen. Remember that even a change of eyeline so that a character seems to be looking in a different direction is enough to render the shot very awkward.

Continuity of time and action must also be controlled. To take an obvious example, if an interviewee is smoking a cigarette or wearing a hat or spectacles which are sometimes on and sometimes off, then it is madness for the cameraman to ignore the implications for the editor. Such details should not dictate the style of shooting and cutting, but they have to be taken into consideration. Otherwise the audience may be distracted from the actual subject of the scene. More problematic is the continuity involved in shooting a meal, especially where there are several courses, a lot of drinking and maybe even waiters who are sometimes in shot and sometimes not.

5   The wide shot to establish a scene is often crucial. There are very few situations where the environment in which a scene is taking place can be ignored even if, once established, it can then be forgotten. The 'frame' in which any film exists is never the 'ideal' that a painter chooses. There is a sense in which Magritte's attempts to prevent the conventions of the frame dominating our perception has a corollary in film. Unless the whole visual context of events is shown, an audience will always feel that there is something beyond the edge of the frame which it is being prevented from seeing (the disembodied questioner is an example). The editor is also helped if he does not have to worry about the geography of a scene once it has been established. If, for instance, a room with a door is established, the noise of it opening and closing off screen does not disorientate the viewer, who actually 'sees' it happening, having already recorded its position. More specific objects, such as machinery that is making a distinct noise, are also best established rather than being allowed to become a nagging question-mark beyond the frame. The reverse of this principle can also be true. The isolation of a person in close-up may be necessary if the activity around him or her is more interesting visually. In such a case it may be best to frustrate the audience's desire to see the whole environment or to save it to a point when the surroundings become relevant. I can never understand why one is occasionally shown a wide shot of the expert standing in front of the painting he is talking about, and then a close-up of him instead of the painting itself while he continues talking about it.

6   Many of the problems in cutting documentaries spring from a tendency to shoot too close. There is often a good reason: sometimes the surroundings prevent the possibility of a wider shot; unless the subject has been 'miked', a noisy background may make it imperative to get a close visual to allow the mike to be positioned near enough – but out of sight – for a usable recording. However, television tends to encourage the idea that the close-up is inherently superior to a more inclusive framing. It is the fact that the close-up excludes so much that gives the editor his problems. Unless the function of the shot is purely interview, in neutral surroundings, the background always contains some relevance. The guideline should be to attempt always to contain all relevant visual information within the frame. Otherwise the editor will continually complain that he cannot see what the subject is talking about or that he is forced to cut away to show relevant things. A good example is the situation where, say, the spokesman for a group is holding forth and we can see his sentiments confirmed (or not!) on the faces of his comrades. This is far superior to the cutaway of one of them nodding, which is now given no more credibility than it deserves. There is also much symbolic

mileage to be gained from placing people in their working environment: the executive behind his desk, the worker at his lathe, the teacher at the blackboard. Of course, there is a danger in oversimplifying the validity of the evidence conveyed by the context in which people are filmed – a bad teacher can look just as impressive in front of a blackboard as a good one – but it is worth conveying that the film has not taken the subjects out of their normal context.

7   To judge how much of the available visual information should be contained within a shot, the good documentary cameraman uses his other eye (and both his ears) just as much if not more than the one that is jammed up against the viewfinder. Unless you are looking and listening beyond the frame, every reaction to a change in focus of interest in a scene will result in a badly executed movement that happens too late. It may also cause the frame you are holding to be indeterminate.

A simple experiment proves the point. When you next find yourself in an environment where people are engaged in some kind of activity and also conversing, put some cotton wool in your ears, close one eye and use your hand as a substitute for looking through a viewfinder. Then ask yourself what criteria are available to you for judging the frame you should hold. The one eye, restricted of course to the normal angle of view through a lens, has no perspective except its own narrow, silent, arbitrary frame. You have no way of knowing why people are doing things, who is talking to whom or what is likely to happen next, if you use the camera as a visual vacuum cleaner. If you attempt to cut the footage obtained you will not know where to start. It is not easy to use your other eye, nor is it easy to maintain an alert hearing function, but both must be learned if you are to produce footage that has a feeling for the events portrayed, rather than some alien, covert, private pattern known only to a one-eyed, deaf, mindless machine!

8   At the other extreme you must be aware of relevant details. Usually after the main body of shooting is over it is very valuable to consider whether objects that have been referred to have been sufficiently well covered in the material. If not, it is important that the way they are then covered has either the original perspective of the camera – if a dominant shooting position has been maintained – or that they are seen as 'point-of-view' shots of the person who has referred to them on camera. The lack of such details can often prevent the construction of a satisfactory sequence.

The cardinal sin in documentary is to be filming without a real purpose; to be amassing footage without really knowing why. It is not unknown for thousands of feet to end up in the cutting room with no more reason than that 'it might be useful'. All this indicates is a complete lack of focus on what the film is really about, and the lazy attitude that presumes the cutting room is a place where miracles are performed on unrelated material. This produces the kind of documentary sewn together only by the ubiquitous narrator whose eccentricity is supposed to justify non-homogeneous sequences and a rag-bag of ideas. The trouble with documentary is that ideas are ten a penny. It is also a pity in a way that we have come to look upon the recording of events such as sport and pageantry as legitimate films. The exception, as with Kon Ichikawa's *Tokyo Olympiad* (1964), proves the rule that it is what the film-maker finds within the event, not the event itself, that legitimizes any film being made of it.

Most ideas for films will occur at first in a general form, but it is only by then asking yourself why? – why a film on that subject? – that you will begin to evaluate the potential. If you are unable to establish a distinct enough attitude to it the idea should be rejected. But if the attitude begins to become coherent then the next question you ask yourself is what? what do I point the camera at? Certainly any self-respecting editor must know the point of view of the director on each and every documentary he cuts. Superimposing an attitude or purpose at the time of cutting is already too late.

THE PROPER USE OF SOUND

It is the perpetual complaint of sound recordists that the aural aspect of filming is the last to be considered. The editor is eventually the one to suffer. It has always seemed strange to me that whereas one person is responsible for the look of a film the quality of its sound is often the divided responsibility of four or five people. At least three will normally have a major influence on the final sound track: the recordist, the editor (or sound editor) and the mixer. Ideally, although it would be impractical, these three roles should be played by one person. Such division of responsibility is an indication of the lack of priority given to sound, and it demands constant vigilance to avoid deleterious consequences. To begin with, the relationship between cameraman and recordist must be a positive one. It is not enough that a cameraman likes working with a particular sound recordist who is compliant with his demands. The needs of both picture and sound must constantly be dealt with in tandem even though getting the right picture has to be the final consideration.

Sync sound
Often the first question that arises is whether to shoot sync or mute. The Italian film industry avoids this decision by post-synchronizing all its feature films. This cuts down shooting schedules but makes its average product fairly unreal, with echoing accoustics on exteriors, badly synchronized dialogue and the most excruciating sound perspectives. There are, of course, exceptions where a totally 'manufactured' sound track has been lovingly created and justifies the technique, especially in films where naturalism is not a prime consideration.

Except where conditions make it impossible, some sort of sync track is invaluable for a number of reasons:

1 The dimension of sound gives a better perspective for evaluating a shot, even though the final choice may be easier viewed mute.
2 Post-synchronization is easier when a guide track is available.
3 If there are instructions on the sound track from the director to the cast they can sometimes be just as useful to the editor.
4 Where there is no dialogue a sync recording may still be helpful. Sync effects are irreplaceable and their quality is never entirely reproducible in the dubbing theatre.
5 If you are aiming for non-naturalistic sound, the sync recording is still valuable as reference and for relative levels.

The reasons why sync shooting may be difficult should be noted if only to placate the editor frustrated by having to cut mute (see Chapter 6 for a full discussion of post-synchronization):

1 *Sounds out of context* If sounds that are inappropriate to the time or place of a scene cannot be excluded from the sync recording, that recording will ultimately have to be replaced. Examples include aircraft passing overhead or mechanical devices used to shoot from (e.g., Indians in canoes shot from a motor boat).

2 *Natural phenomena* Wind and rain, even if they do not prohibit shooting altogether, often make the obtaining of a good recording impossible, especially if there is no way of protecting the microphone.

3 *Camera noise* Where interiors are dominated by glass or similar materials, the noise made by the camera mechanism is often unacceptable, especially if it is impossible to get the microphone far enough away. Even blimped cameras are sometimes too noisy for satisfactory recording indoors.

4 *The nature of the shot* Extreme long shots may make recording difficult although radio microphones can overcome this. Working in tight situations which exclude the recordist are also a problem though pre-setting a microphone position can be a solution.

Wild sound

If for these or any other reasons a sync recording is out of the question, the next best thing is to record a wild track while the camera is rolling, as a guide for cutting. If this too is impossible then the recordist should attempt to get the actors to record a wild track of the dialogue in the same situation immediately after shooting. This has two distinct advantages over post-synchronization: the rhythm, pace and feel of the scene will match that of the performances just given for the camera, and the recording will include the natural atmospheric background to the shot (unless of course the unsuitability of the background was the reason why the scene was not shot sync in the first place). In cases where this option fails too, it is still invaluable to record wild tracks of the background sound, for use by the editor as a realistic support to the post-synchronized dialogue.

Wild tracks are the best yardstick to measure how committed a recordist is to a particular film. It will often be necessary to work against the odds to obtain even the barest minimum of useful sound beyond that recorded while the camera is turning, but the recordist who is prepared to get up early and stay late in order to obtain the imaginative wild tracks earns the eternal gratitude of the editor. Often only the absolutely essential sound is supplied, when if more effort were made it could completely transform material. Two examples from my own experience will suffice. In both films the recordist was the imaginative and professional John Murphy.

A documentary film about Florence, *No Mean City* (1965), directed by Michael Tuchner and edited by Dave King, contained mute material from all over the city. Two shots were particularly evocative – one was a slow tracking shot from a car passing narrow streets; the other was of balloons being released from Piazzale Michelangelo above the city, while

15 Walking shots can make sync recording very difficult: Christopher Gable and Maureen Pryor in Ken Russell's film about Delius, *Song of Summer*

the camera was panning and tilting to reveal the panorama of the city below. Amongst the wild tracks was one, obviously recorded in the heart of the old city, with traffic coming and going in the middle distance and the sound of *arpeggios* being practised on a piano in an upstairs room. This brought the tracking shot to life beautifully as if orchestrated deliberately. The shot from the square needed something to convey the feeling of activity in the square itself and also the atmosphere of the city on the other side of River Arno. The recordist had obtained wild tracks of laughing and squealing children which exactly matched the mood of the balloons drifting upwards, and this was laid to mix through to the distant sounds of the bells of the cathedral and churches of Florence which Murphy had also immaculately recorded. It is this kind of imaginative response to situations that marks out a good recordist.

Two examples from Ken Russell's *Song of Summer* (1968) illustrate an intelligent response to situations in which sync recording was difficult. The first, a hand-held walking shot, prevented the placing of the microphone in a functional position but immediately afterwards the recordist obtained two or three takes of the dialogue as a wild track. With only very minor adjustments these fitted perfectly and no post-synchronization was necessary. In the second, the noise of aircraft prevented a usable recording. Knowing that in this case post-synchronization would be unavoidable, Murphy went to the location at six-thirty the following morning and obtained an atmosphere track and several alternative footstep recordings, using his assistant who walked over the same ground as the performers had the day before.

A less fortunate recordist, the late Bill Meekums, on the BBC's serialization of *The Last of the Mohicans* (1971), directed by David

Maloney, denied the opportunity to record various tracks of canoe paddling at the time of shooting, eventually returned to where the canoes had been left to find that vandals had destroyed and sunk them. It is this kind of unfortunate experience that breaks the conscientious recordist's heart. The laying up of over 2000 separate sounds of paddles did not exactly please my assistant either!

When recording wild tracks it is also worth bearing in mind the length of the scene which they are meant to cover. Often very useful tracks are just not long enough and if they contain identifiable sounds it may be impractical to lay up several transfers of the same section. Perspective is also of great importance. Some adjustment can be made when mixing, but the built-in background to a specific effect often prevents radical alteration of overall level. In any case, perspective is a much more subtle thing than mere differences in level.

In the end, sound is the only element which can add to the essentially two-dimensional feel of an image. Sometimes, of course, in documentaries the roles are reversed: a wild-track interview needs to be illustrated. Even sync interviews may require illustrative material. If you are filming in the natural habitat of the interviewee then material should be available. Such visuals should be simple, direct and economic. They should reinforce or comment on the spoken word so that picture and sound produce a comprehensible synthesis.

PAPERWORK

The most irritating aspect of shooting is the need for several kinds of paperwork. When you are struggling to translate your script or thoughts into pictures and sounds, the last thing you want to do is to stop and make detailed notes of everything. However, if you don't you are storing up considerable trouble for the editing stage. Camera sheets, sound reports, continuity notes, shot lists and marked-up scripts all have a useful function:

Camera sheet
As can be seen from the example, a considerable amount of information is available to the editor from a well filled-in camera sheet or negative report. If, as is usual with 16 mm film, all footage is printed, it is possible from this sheet to determine the cameraman's preferred take of each slate. The question sometimes arises as to whether there is any discrepancy between the preferences of cameraman and director: it is unusual for the two of them to be in accord on every slate.

Sound report
This is a simpler document than the above, but the two taken together are invaluable, especially when synchronizing rushes. The example lists where slates are sync or wild, what wild tracks have been obtained and to what slates they refer, and the general comments of the recordist as to the usefulness of each recording.

Continuity notes
On dramatic films it is usual practice to supply these detailed notes of the nature of each shot. They include the director's own preferences for takes

PRODUCTION COMPANY *THE NATIONAL FILM SCHOOL* Nº 04827
DATE *5·3·81*   PRODUCTION *'HIATUS'*
CAMERAMAN *P·SARGENT*   DIRECTOR *R·CRITTENDEN*
LABORATORY *DENHAM*   EMULSION DETAILS *EASTMAN 7247*

MUTE NEGATIVE REPORT

ROLL No.	SLATE No.	1	2	3	4	5	6	7	8	REMARKS	TOTAL
1	1	✓	✓	(✓)	(✓)					DAY/INT.	60'
	2	(✓)								MUTE	75'
	3	✓	(✓)								97'
	4	(✓)	(✓)								112'
	5	✓	✓	(✓)	✓	(✓)				↓	157'
2	6	(✓)	✓							DAY/EXT.	72'
	7	(✓)									81'
	8	(✓)	✓	(✓)							96'
	9	✓	(✓)								113'
	10	(✓)									121'
	11	(✓)	(✓)							MUTE	160'
	12	✓	✓	✓	(✓)						194'
	13	(✓)								MUTE-RUNOUT	200'
3	14	(✓)	✓							NIGHT/EXT.	20'
	15	(✓)									55'
	16	✓	(✓)	✓							71'
	17	(✓)									124'
	18	(✓)	(✓)								133'
	19	✓	✓	(✓)							151'
	20	(✓)	(✓)	(✓)						↓	180'

PRINT CIRCLED TAKES ONLY

LABORATORY INSTRUCTIONS:

SUPPLY ONE-LIGHT COLOUR RUSH PRINT AND DELIVER TO STUDIOS

TO-DAYS TOTAL 537'
" " WASTE 63'
PREVIOUS TOTAL —
TOTAL USED 600

TOTAL CANS: 3

Report Sheets by
SAMUELSON FILM SERVICE LIMITED

16 Negative report or camera sheet: the circled takes are the ones the cameraman considers usable

<table>
<tr><td colspan="2">NATIONAL FILM SCHOOL</td></tr>
</table>

SOUND REPORT	
ROLL NO.	*3*

PRODUCTION *OPEN SPACES-SCOTT THOMAS*

PROD. No. *NONE*   DATE *6/3/81*

CAMERA *ECLAIR*   24 (25) f.p.s.

RECORDER *NAGRA 4·2*   3¾ (7½) 15 i.p.s.

PULSE	CABLE	TRANSFER
(50 cps)	(CRYSTAL)	(16 mm)
60 cps	MAINS	35 mm

TONE   AT *8db*

RECORDIST *GARETH HAYWOOD*

SLATE	TAKE	REMARKS
1	*1*	
	2	*False start-Sync to 2nd Clap*
	3	
2	*1*	
	2	*N.G. Aircraft*
	3	
	4	
W/T 1	*1*	*TO Cover slate 1*
	2	
ATMOS TRACK to Cover Slates 1		*and 2*
3	*1*	*low level-please increase*
	2	*level on transfer*
4	*1*	*BOE*
	2	
	3	
	4	*No slate - Camera run out*
W/T2	*1*	*[N.G.] for slate 4*
	2	*"Goodbye Peter"*
	3	*N.G.*
	4	
W/T 3	*1*	*Door slam (slate 4)*
	2	*" " "*

17 On this sound report, W/T means wild track, N.G. means no good, and BOE means board on end (i.e. that the clapperboard is inserted at the end of the shot)

which, as was said, may be at variance with the preferences of cameraman and/or sound recordist. Continuity notes also give reasons why takes are not good enough (sometimes this does not prevent the take being used, especially if the section the editor wishes to incorporate in his cut is not affected by the fault).

Shot lists
These are really the equivalent of continuity notes for documentaries, but are not always available to the editor, who may decide to make his own as he logs his rushes (see p. 68). Efficiently produced shot lists are really

PRODUCTION VENOM

DATE: 29.10.80

CAMERAS & SET UPS:

SET: Int.Living room

pfx21 : 32mm ; 8'8" ; t4.

TIME SHOT: Night

SCREENTIME: 00.10s

WEATHER: n.a.

24fps sync

Scene No.   97 √ut.

Slate No.   151

Action & Dialogue:

2-SHOT JACMEL & DAVE TRACK BACK TO CLOSER 2-SHOT.

M.W.S. shooting towards the tv wall with JACMEL standing f.g.
holding the curtains back with his th rh - gun in his lh -
focus on DAVE in the b.g. holding his shotgun across his chest
Track back as DAVE walks up to JACMEL.   Both look down r - l
to street. JACMEL replaces drape.   Cut

CHAT
DAVE: THEY'RE TAKING THE CAR   (by the window)
          THEY'RE TAKING THE CAR. (next to Jacmel and shouting).
                                    Cut

Take 1 : n.g. : Ok Dave does NOT shout on this one
Take 2 : n.g. : but OK
take 3 : PRINT : OK (10s)
Take 4 : PRINT : OK (10s)

18 The OK takes at the bottom of these continuity notes indicate the director's preference

a diary of the shoot which contain much information not available from any other source and often details that would have been forgotten had they not been committed to paper at the time of shooting.

Marked-up script
As the example shows, this is a translation of the continuity notes into a script that gives the editor a graphic guide to the way each scene is covered and an instant reference to the alternatives available to him at any moment. (See p. 67.)

In this way paperwork can give the editor much necessary information. The guideline when completing such forms should be the question: what information should the editor have which is not obvious from the material itself? After all is said and done, weeks, maybe months, of effort by numerous people are finally reduced to a pile of cans full of celluloid and magnetic film. It makes sense to ensure that the person who is supposed to breathe life into that footage should be given all the support possible.

Strand/Series Title	OMNIBUS			SHOOTING ORDER SHOT LIST (continued)			
Programme Title	TOO MUCH REALITY????					Page No.	6
Episode/ Sub. Title							
Project Number	06349/9003						
Programme Identificat'n Number							

Camera Roll No.	Slate No.	Take	Description	Sound	Tape No.	Duration
14	14	5	<u>Exterior</u>: Pan from pit wheel to Joris and Les walking across yard and into wheel shaft building	s		45"
		6	<u>Interior</u>: Pnt. Wheel shaft. Pan down from wheel head to Joris and Les talking about the shaft (½ mile deep!). at 1'45" pan up to wheel shaft. (not a lot of activity as wheel not moving)	s		2'05"
	14 no board	7	<u>Exterior</u>: LS Joris and Les walking to camera towards slag heap. Pan round as passes camera. @ 2'00" pan off to slag heap (ng at 2'15 as roll run out on pan)	s		2'15"
15	15	1eb	<u>Cutaway</u> slag heap. CS coal coming out of shaft, pan right to truck moving up and down. <u>Wildtrack</u> to cover	m	8	2'00"
	15	2eb	<u>Interior</u>: LAMP ROOM. Looking down between lockers. LS Joris and Les talking. @ 1'30" pan left to man at lamp locker. _Wildtrack_ on end of sound take	s		1'50"
	15	3eb	<u>Interior</u> LS looking down side of lockers, Joris and Les talking to younger man. Man explains equipment to Joris	s	8 &	2'30"
	15	4eb	LS looking down side of lockers. Pan left as Sarah, Joris and Les talking - pan left off to lockers. At 2'30 pan to look down side of lockers	s	8 &	3'30"
16	16	1	<u>Exterior</u>: Men coming up from pit in their orange overalls and walk across yard (to lamp room) towards camera. Joris and Les talking to oen of the 'orange men'. Hold on 3-shot, MS. at 2'00" MS pan right to group sitting/talking by rose beds. Pan left at 3'00P to 3-shot MS Pan right with 'orange man' as he walks behind them, and then hold on group sitting. Group get up and walk off. at 5'15 pan left back to Joris, etc. on MS (see transcripts)	s	B	6'00"

19 This shot list is from a BBC documentary film on Joris Ivens, the famous documentary maker, directed by Sarah Boston

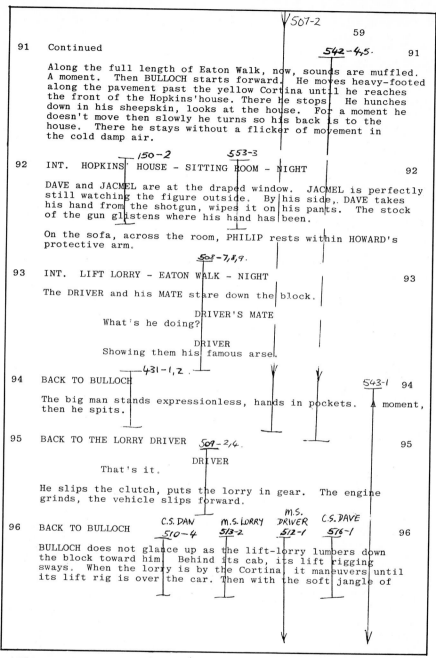

507-2

59

91   Continued   542-4,5.   91

    Along the full length of Eaton Walk, now, sounds are muffled.
A moment. Then BULLOCH starts forward. He moves heavy-footed
along the pavement past the yellow Cortina until he reaches
the front of the Hopkins'house. There he stops. He hunches
down in his sheepskin, looks at the house. For a moment he
doesn't move then slowly he turns so his back is to the
house. There he stays without a flicker of movement in
the cold damp air.

          150-2   553-3

92   INT. HOPKINS' HOUSE - SITTING ROOM - NIGHT   92

    DAVE and JACMEL are at the draped window. JACMEL is perfectly
still watching the figure outside. By his side, DAVE takes
his hand from the shotgun, wipes it on his pants. The stock
of the gun glistens where his hand has been.

On the sofa, across the room, PHILIP rests within HOWARD's
protective arm.

          508-7,8,9.

93   INT.   LIFT LORRY - EATON WALK - NIGHT   93

    The DRIVER and his MATE stare down the block.

                DRIVER'S MATE
         What's he doing?

                 DRIVER
        Showing them his famous arse.

        431-1,2.

94   BACK TO BULLOCH   543-1   94

    The big man stands expressionless, hands in pockets. A moment,
then he spits.

95   BACK TO THE LORRY DRIVER   509-2,4.   95

                 DRIVER
         That's it.

He slips the clutch, puts the lorry in gear. The engine
grinds, the vehicle slips forward.

                           m.S.
            C.S. DAN   M.S. LORRY DRIVER C.S. DAVE
96   BACK TO BULLOCH   510-4   513-2   512-1   516-1   96

    BULLOCH does not glance up as the lift-lorry lumbers down
the block toward him. Behind its cab, its lift rigging
sways. When the lorry is by the Cortina, it maneuvers until
its lift rig is over the car. Then with the soft jangle of

20 This page of marked-up script not only tells the editor which slates cover each section
of a scene, but also which are the chosen takes

3   The cutting room and editing equipment

In *The Parade's Gone By* (1968) Kevin Brownlow chronicled the early days of editing thus: 'Editing in common with other aspects of techniques settled down to a solid professionalism around 1918. Astonishingly most editors worked without the animated viewers considered essential today. They cut in the hand. Modern film editors are baffled by this; how could they possibly judge the pace or the rhythm?'

He goes on to describe how 'cutting in the hand' only died out when sound brought synchronization problems, and quotes Bebe Daniels's comment on Moviolas, the new editing machines: 'The old cutters would not use them – They were like old cooks who refused to use pressure cookers.'

Of course, it is still true that the only really essential pieces of equipment for cutting are a pair of scissors, a razor blade, glue, a light-box, a pair of rewinds and a projector. It must be remembered that for many years editors always cut on 35 mm and each frame was visible to the naked eye. Matching action on 35 mm is still sometimes most easily done by aligning the frames to be cut together in the hand over a light-box; and the beauty of the projector as the only viewing device is precisely that you are forced to *watch* the film rather than having constantly to stop and start to analyse each frame separately. The establishment of good pace, rhythm and, indeed, structure depends upon building up a sense of whole sequences, and avoiding a concern with the static moment that exists at each cut.

So what do contemporary editors surround themselves with, and how do you best use the space allotted for cutting a film? These are questions

21 The sophistication of the editor's environment has developed considerably since this portrayal of a cutting room in 1920 in Lescarboura's *Behind the Motion Picture Screen*

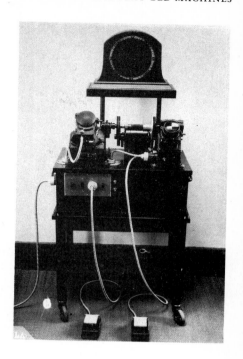

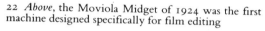
22 *Above*, the Moviola Midget of 1924 was the first machine designed specifically for film editing

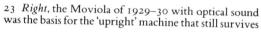
23 *Right*, the Moviola of 1929–30 with optical sound was the basis for the 'upright' machine that still survives

worth considering if only to avoid the incredible chaos pictured in Austin C. Lescarboura's *Behind the Motion Picture Screen* (1920), where editing merits half a page in a 420-page book!

UPRIGHT AND FLAT-BED MACHINES

Until the last twenty years, editing technology was the poor relation, the least considered of the tools of the trade. It would have been even worse had it not been for Iwan Serurier who invented the Moviola. As can be seen from the illustrations, this machine has changed very little in its basic design, especially since it was first adapted for sound in 1929. It is a little recognized fact that no technology is neutral in its effect on the process for which it is designed. The Moviola is an outstanding example of a machine dictating attitudes to, and the product of, the craft it is used for.

The development of flat-bed or table editing machines (e.g. Steenbeck, KEM and Prevost), using a continuous prism movement, has shown that there are no innate reasons why the characteristics of the Moviola are essential to editing. The intermittent motion of the picture head, the vertical movement, the small screen and the standing position for operating are all part of a mode that has been abandoned in the alternative design.

The characteristics of the Moviola may or may not have been arrived at consciously. Since the camera and projector pre-dated editing machinery, it was their design detail that provided the original reference point for the design of the Moviola; indeed, the earliest machines were simply crude adaptations of the mechanisms of cameras and projectors. We must also remember that the designer had in mind the habitual

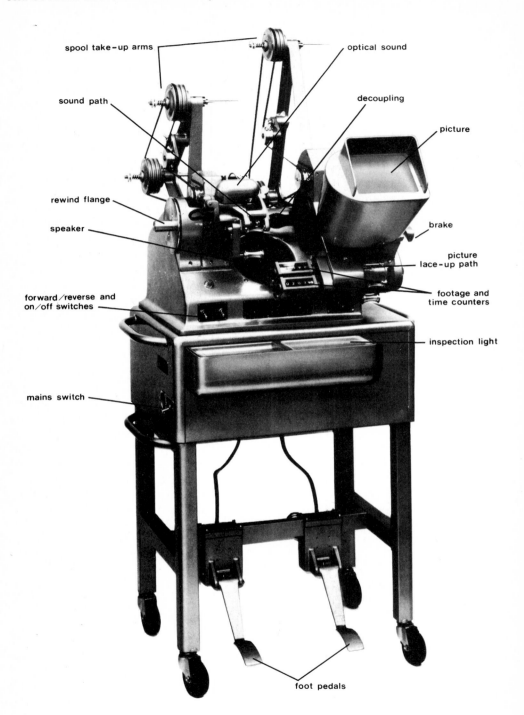

spool take-up arms

optical sound

sound path

decoupling

picture

rewind flange

brake

speaker

picture
lace-up path

forward/reverse and
on/off switches

footage and
time counters

inspection light

mains switch

foot pedals

24 The standard 35 mm Moviola. Both the picture- and sound-head clamps are easily lifted for the film to be inserted. The spool take-up arms are not normally used, so very short lengths of film can be run. Cutting marks on the film are easily made as the picture head swivels away while the clamp that holds the film in place remains fixed

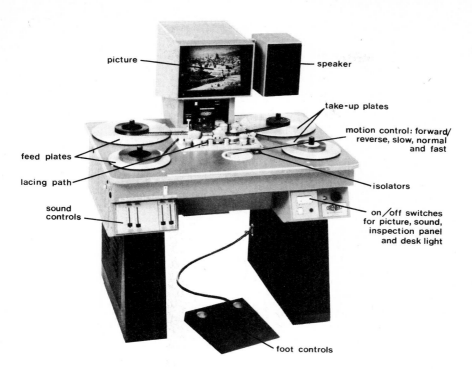

picture — — speaker

take-up plates

motion control: forward/
reverse, slow, normal
and fast

feed plates —

lacing path —

isolators

sound
controls —

on/off switches
for picture, sound,
inspection panel
and desk light

foot controls

25 A standard 16 mm Steenbeck with large picture display and simple controls. Like all flat-beds it uses continuous motion and is notable for its quietness. The lacing path is not complicated although several feet of film are required to thread from feed to take-up plates

cutting method – in the hand, over a light-box – and assumed he was producing an occasional aid to the editing process and not a replacement for the already established routine. The Moviola was conceived of as a way of instantly checking a few feet of film which also, unintentionally, gave editors an opportunity to match action and re-action in a way not available in the hand. It is one thing to make a cut that allows a movement to continue over it; it is quite another to determine, by running the two shots several times through a mechanism at correct film speed, when is the best moment to match that movement. It has been argued that rhythm and pacing were mastered by silent editors to such an extent that they could 'see' the moving image at the correct speed in the hand! However, I am sure the advent of the Moviola gave editors a distinct advantage in gauging the rhythm of cutting. Once established in the 1930s the Moviola soon dictated much more than the mechanics of cutting: the cutting room was designed around it, indeed the original bench with synchronizer and rewinds was an integral part of Moviola-style cutting; but the most significant effect of the Moviola, which is still relevant today, was the way it encouraged editors to relate to their material. Editing at the Moviola, as is obvious from a few moments of observation, is a positive, even aggressive, operation. You can sense that the editor feels an almost physical challenge as the film rattles back and forth through the gate. The editor stands in a dominating fashion slapping

26 A Super 8 MKM flat-bed, providing professional technology for an amateur gauge. (Similar machines are also available from other manufacturers)

and slamming pieces in and out of the mechanism like a lion-tamer trying to prove who is really King of the Editing Jungle! You can imagine Sam Peckinpah or Howard Hawks exercising on a Moviola on getting out of bed in the morning rather than indulging in callisthenics. Indeed, it's a man's world at the Moviola (although, in my opinion, the best editor at the Moviola is a woman, Dede Allen).

Contrast this with a visit to an established cutting room in Germany where a Steenbeck or another flat-bed machine is holding court. You enter a world of soft lights and ample women with coffee on tap and vases of flowers decorating the carpeted room. The film runs silently

27 A 16mm KEM with 8 plates, enabling the running of three pictures with one sound track

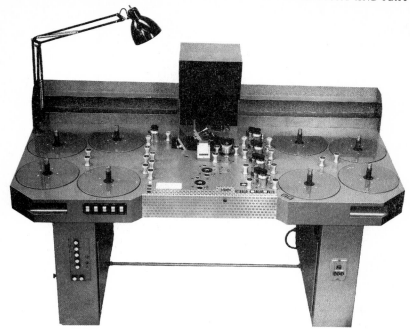

28 Prevost editing machines are also available in many forms. This model allows three sound tracks and one picture for either 35 mm or 16 mm

back and forth with only the occasional click signifying a change of direction. You hear the odd comment, hardly above a whisper, between director and editor. You wonder why your teeth are beginning to ache, until you realize that the ambience reminds you of nothing so much as your dentist's surgery, with everything calculated to prevent the director's ulcers flaring up!

This contrast is of greater significance than most people realize. Neither type of machine actually dictates such an extreme and different attitude to cutting, but each encourages a particular mode of working. It is often argued that the Moviola is best suited to dramatic films shot for continuity cutting, and the flat-bed machine to certain kinds of documentary.

In some circles the flat-bed machine is still considered to be useful only for viewing. It seems likely that this was their only expected function when first produced, especially considering their kindness to film, the fact that they allow show copies and reversal masters to be run with little risk of damage (although this is not normally recommended). This was especially true when 35 mm was the only recognized professional gauge. With the advent of 16 mm a gentler machine than the Moviola was desirable (in a sense the Moviola relied on the toughness of 35 mm for its operation) and the flat-bed machines came into their own. Since then, the two types have become real alternatives – a fact recognized by the Moviola Company themselves when they began to produce their own flat-bed machine a few years ago.

It remains true, however, that editors usually espouse one type as the only really effective editing device. Sometimes the editor's temperament is as much a deciding factor as either a rational analysis of the way the

29 The Moviola flat-bed is a sophisticated machine. This example takes two sound tracks and one picture

machines function or of the kind of films they are working on. Even if you have no choice as to which kind of machine you will use, it is as well to be aware of the advantages and disadvantages of both. As you can imagine, I launch into such a comparison with considerable trepidation knowing that with each statement at least 50 per cent of editors will be gnashing their teeth! I shall consequently endeavour to concentrate on differences that arise out of the mechanical operation and to allow your own personal experience to determine your preference. The important thing is not to ignore the effects of working with one or other type of machine. There are, of course, many makes of editing machine besides the Moviola and Steenbeck, but most exhibit the characteristics of one or other type.

	MOVIOLA (upright machine)	STEENBECK (flat-bed or table machine)
Lacing path	Simple and very short	Easy but needs several feet of film
Picture	Bright but limited viewing	Large enough to allow viewing by several people
Sound	Satisfactory	Satisfactory

Variable speed	Fast forward and reverse on picture only	4–50 frames per second forward and reverse in sync (some faster)
Kindness to film	Only suitable for cutting copy	Possible to run show copies
Speed of operation	Very fast if used with synchronizer and rewinds	Not so easy to manipulate for complex cutting
Marking up	Simple, quick, exact	Simple and quick but position of frame over sound head needs watching
Cutting	By removing from gate	Rewound to one side of gate
Reliability	Requires careful maintenance	Rewards proper use

THE SYNCHRONIZER

The choice of editing machinery has however become more complicated with the development of the picture-synchronizer (now marketed in its new and more sophisticated form as the Compeditor).

For many years the synchronizer was an aid to editing – its use, combined with the Moviola, dominated cutting-room practice in Hollywood and elsewhere until the advent of the flat-bed machine. It began life, as its name implies, as a reliable way of keeping the film in synchronization. Several revolving wheels with teeth to engage the film perforations, and a clamping device to hold the film when engaged, allowed the cut film to be lined up and run through to check and retain sync. The most obvious use for the original synchronizer was to match the original negative or reversal master to the cutting copy before printing the final film but, once sound heads had been added, much more elaborate use of the device became feasible.

With 35 mm film, a light-box underneath the synchronizer provided an adequate means of reference to the individual picture frame. With 16 mm this was impossible. The growth of 16 mm as the predominant gauge used in television, especially in Europe, encouraged the idea that the synchronizer could become a more useful device if fitted with a means of viewing the picture. Once this was achieved it was a small step to incorporate a motor to allow picture and sound to be run at normal sync speed. Enlargement of the picture and the facility to decouple either the picture gang from the sound or one of the sound tracks from the others have produced a very flexible machine – good enough for editors to choose to work exclusively without other aids except when wishing to view cut film comfortably.

More complicated editing can be greatly assisted by the use of 'pic-syncs' with additional picture or sound tracks. These are available in all types but three sound tracks are standard to picture synchronizers. Films that have been shot on several cameras simultaneously or where more than one sound track is important to the cutting, demand more elaborate facilities, but the seductive nature of over-sophistication should be guarded against. Laying more than one sound track early in the cutting

30 A classic four-way Moviola
35 mm synchronizer. The simple
clamping device allows for swift
insertion and removal of film

process can inhibit the kind of complex consideration of alternatives that
is usually necessary, since doing so requires re-vamping too many
elements. I can remember falling into the trap of laying a music track
against a sync dialogue sequence, because it was being played on a radio
in shot. I found that it required a lot of discipline to remain aware of the
rhythm that the dialogue and dramatic action suggested when the music
had its own internal rhythm and form. Rather than hankering after
special equipment, it is much more important to be able to see and hear
your picture and sound well and to know your machine is reliable.

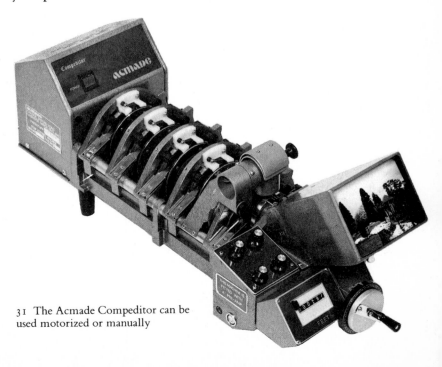

31 The Acmade Compeditor can be
used motorized or manually

MAGNETIC SOUND AND TAPE JOINERS

The heyday of the Moviola included two other important elements which have since been superseded: optical sound and cement joiners or splicers. It was the era of the level cut (i.e. where picture and sound were almost always cut parallel with each other), and a time when each cut was a real commitment since, with the use of cement joiners, frames were lost each time a cut was made. The only ways to restore shots to their original form was either to insert frames of 'build-up' or to reprint: the one unsatisfactory because you could no longer see the entire shot, the other costly and time-consuming. Optical sound had the advantage over magnetic sound of being visible, cutting tight to a modulation was easier, and experienced editors became able to read simple and common words from the appearance of the track, but again once cut there was no easy way of restoring that particular take.

Magnetic film is an oxide-coated base, originally celluloid but now more frequently polyester, on to which the sound recording is transferred from the original $\frac{1}{4}$-in. tapes. It is perforated like photographic film for use on editing machines, projectors and other equipment for reproduction. The actual sound-track area is a very narrow band positioned in the centre or sometimes on the edge opposite to the perforations. In 35 mm magnetic film is often striped rather than fully coated with oxide, saving cost in raw material. Tape joiners are simple devices for cutting and splicing. As they do not create an overlap at the join, no frames are lost, which gives them a great advantage over cement joiners.

Magnetic track and tape joiners have less drawbacks than their predecessors but they do still have shortcomings. Magnetic track is in theory reusable but in practice very little gets used again due to wear and the disadvantage of joins. Tape joiners encourage experimentation in

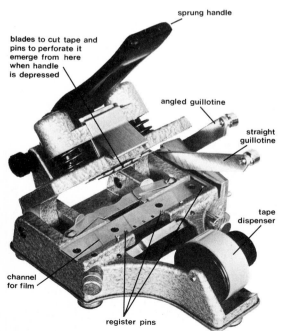

sprung handle

blades to cut tape and pins to perforate it emerge from here when handle is depressed

angled guillotine

straight guillotine

tape dispenser

channel for film

register pins

32 The tape joiner. Although different makes vary in detail the basic mechanism consists of a channel for registering the film, a guillotine, a tape dispenser and a sprung device for perforating the tape once it is applied to the sections of film. The additional diagonal guillotine is for cutting sound to avoid a bump or click at the join

cutting, but being able to restore shots is a mixed blessing. Too many joins can make it impossible to judge the cutting – especially when projected – as each join shudders through the gate and you are more conscious of tape joins than the cuts themselves. Both magnetic track and tape joins are subject to deterioration. It is essential to avoid running your track over sound heads at speed and under tension any more than is absolutely necessary. Unless you are working in features, the cutting track will usually be used when mixing and, unless you lay up re-transfers from the original $\frac{1}{4}$-in. tape, excessive wear will be noticeable in the quality of the final sound track. Tension will also eventually stretch the joins both on picture and sound, the results of which can be disastrous. It may become necessary to remake *and* back the joins in the picture before projecting, and to remake the joins in the sound track. In the latter case, even if there is no accident while running the track, there will be audible 'drop-outs' where gaps have appeared in the track. It is also possible to lose sync because bad joins enlarge or diminish the 'loop' on the projector or cause slippage on the sound reproducers. For all these reasons much care and attention should be given to the making of tape joins.

THE SYNC BENCH

The bench is a remnant of the days when no mechanical devices existed for editing, but its usefulness has been sustained. If you have any say in the dimensions and layout of this so-called sync bench, keep in mind the following criteria that relate to the way it is used:

1   Its height should be convenient for working both standing and sitting.
2   Its depth should be sufficient for a multiple synchronizer, for the storage of film at the back and for the tape joiner to sit comfortably at the front.
3   The length should allow rewinds at each end with extra space for a horse (if used) on the left – but it should not be too long for convenient handling from the centre.
4   There should be some kind of backing board to keep material from falling off; this can incorporate a trough for rolls of film.
5   There should be holes cut out of the bench, with hooks for the insertion of bags, to allow rewinding or winding on without having to take up the resultant slack.
6   The working surface should be smooth, light in colour and easily cleanable to avoid unnecessary damage to your film.
7   The centrepiece can include a light-box to allow close examination of sections of film, although the picture synchronizer has made this virtually redundant except when cutting negative or master material.
8   The legs and cross-supports should be strong enough for strenuous working although, for comfort, nothing in the construction should prevent one sitting close to the working surface.
9   The front central section can include an inset plastic measuring strip, divided into units the length of frames, which is invaluable for marking up opticals.

The illustration complies with most of these criteria and shows how rewinds, bags and synchronizer combine to make this simple bench the

33 An Acmade sync bench which incorporates the Compeditor (*ill. 31*)

hub of much cutting-room activity (although you will notice from the example of the cutting-room layout in ill. 36 that the sync bench is by no means a universal device).

THE TRIM BIN AND OTHER ACCESSORIES

Perhaps the most ubiquitous gadget is the trim bin. This primitive apparatus is the lazy editor's filing system. Even when elaborated with light panels and clips instead of nails it is still only useful if treated with a degree of scepticism. A trim bin has a limited capacity: trims hung in it should always be returned to their original cans at regular intervals. In this way the trim bin can be a helpful aid through each phase of cutting. If you let the amount of material on it get out of hand, there is much less chance of finding those important few frames that you are bound to need in a hurry.

Just as essential to a well-managed editing suite are boxes or cans for the material, all of which must be clearly labelled in a way that can be seen at a glance and also stacked so that a particular one can be removed from the shelf easily and without disturbing any others. The best way of labelling is with camera tape: write the identification in felt-tip pen on two pieces of tape and attach one to the side and one to the lid of the box or can. The essential information should include title, picture and/or track, print or negative, slate numbers and whether the box or can contains cutting copy, trims or spares.

The cutting room needs a considerable number of other accessories in order to function efficiently. One of the simplest but most essential items are cores or bobbins, without which the sections of film are difficult to handle, especially when broken down into short lengths. To use the rewinds on the sync bench requires split spools, springs, clamps and spacers. These should be guarded with your life to avoid the inconvenience of working with too few spools.

During cutting, film needs to be clearly identified. The standard device for marking film itself is wax pencil or chinagraph. Unlike most alternatives, this marks film easily, the mark is just as easily removed and it does not scratch the emulsion. The most useful colours are black, red, yellow and white – allowing for clear marking on print, magnetic track, spacing and clear film. When marking up leaders for the beginning and end of rolls, it is convenient to use felt-tip pens of the variety used for poster lettering. It is important to obtain the kind which produces a reasonably indelible mark especially when writing on the base of white spacer whose shiny surface tends to reject most inks.

Spacer and leaders are also essential in the cutting room. Spacer can, of course, be any waste film, though ideally single perforation white spacer is the best (single perforation to ensure it is inserted into picture and sound-track rolls the right way round for machines and projectors, and white to allow the clearest possible marking). Standard leaders (or, according to the specific function, projection leaders, academy leaders, dubbing leaders and printer leaders) are all used to cue the start of a roll of film. It is possible to use marked-up spacer as a substitute leader but eventually a proper leader will have to be used.

Production companies, television stations and laboratories all produce different species of leader but they universally exhibit the basic markings which were established by the American Academy of Motion Picture Arts and Sciences in the 1930s. Working from the head inwards, a plain section for identification is followed by some kind of start-mark for synchronous lacing in the projector or editing machine – this mark is usually twelve 35mm feet from the first frame of picture, although television often works with a fifteen-foot equivalent. After this there is a count-down leader with windows showing the number of feet decreasing progressively to three (3). At this point the numbers stop to ensure that projectionists can allow the image to reach the screen without revealing further numbers, ensuring a neat change-over between reels.

If such a leader is attached to your cutting-copy picture all the sound track needs is a sync mark opposite the start, identification on the front and a sync bleep at the '3'. This device allows for positive synchronization where there may be variable run-up speeds between projector and sound reproducers, and gives the laboratory a reference point when marrying picture and sound into a combined print. The bleep consists of one frame of thousand-cycle tone and can be obtained from any dubbing theatre or transfer suite.

The cutting room does not require an abundance of paper beyond the various information sheets that we talked about in the last chapter (see p. 40). The log book will be dealt with in chapter 4. It is useful to have a film footage/time conversion chart but remember they exist for 24 *and* 25 frames per second running speeds and you must refer to the right one. As a general guide key footages are shown in the table opposite. It is also worth having a laboratory price list (as long as it is current!) A constant reminder of the cost of reprints should make you more careful when handling the material. Also any information on laboratory processes, especially an optical chart, can be helpful. Laboratories also supply a specially designed optical order pad – it is as well to follow this since you will then be giving that department the information they require in the form they are used to.

Feet	35 mm (16 frames per foot)		16 mm (40 frames per foot)	
	24 f.p.s. Min. Sec.	25 f.p.s. Min. Sec.	24 f.p.s. Min. Sec.	25 f.p.s. Min. Sec.
1	0.7	0.6	1.7	1.6
2	1.3	1.3	3.3	3.2
3	2.0	1.9	5.0	4.8
4	2.7	2.6	6.7	6.4
5	3.3	3.2	8.3	8.0
6	4.0	3.9	10.0	9.6
7	4.7	4.4	11.7	11.2
8	5.3	5.1	13.3	12.8
9	6.0	5.8	15.0	14.4
10	6.7	6.4	16.7	16.0
20	13.3	12.8	33.3	32.0
30	20.0	19.2	50.0	48.0
40	26.7	25.7	1.06.7	1.04.0
50	33.3	32.0	1.23.3	1.20.0
60	40.0	38.4	1.40.0	1.36.0
70	46.7	44.9	1.56.7	1.52.0
80	53.3	51.2	2.13.3	2.08.0
90	1.00.0	57.6	2.30.0	2.24.0
100	1.06.7	1.04.0	2.46.7	2.40.0
200	2.13.3	2.08.0	5.33.3	5.20.0
300	3.20.0	3.12.1	8.20.0	8.00.0
400	4.26.7	4.16.0	11.06.7	10.40.0
500	5.33.3	5.20.0	13.53.3	13.20.0
600	6.40.0	6.24.0	16.40.0	16.00.0
700	7.46.7	7.28.0	19.26.7	18.40.0
800	8.53.3	8.32.0	22.13.3	21.20.0
900	10.00.0	9.36.0	25.00.0	24.00.0
1000	11.06.7	10.40.0	27.46.7	26.40.0

34 Film footage conversion chart. This contains all measurements necessary to calculate the time equivalence of any footage. Sound-recording studios always work to 35 mm feet to ensure maximum accuracy. Dubbing or mixing charts must therefore show 35 mm footages, so you must ensure that your equipment incorporates a counter that registers one foot per 16 frames. Remember that timing your film with a stop watch will only be accurate if your editing machine is running at the correct speed

It is also necessary to have the following consumables: joining tape, camera tape, cleaning fluid, spare bulbs (and fuses) for equipment, dusters, anti-static cloths for dry-cleaning film, rubber bands and/or paper clips for securing pieces of film.

Ideally the room should have good ventilation, a subdued light source for viewing, venetian or roller blinds for the windows, a rewind bench to avoid having to rewind on the editing machine, and chairs of adjustable height. The floors, walls and working surfaces should be easy to clean, although some people prefer carpeted floors to reduce ambient noise. Above all the best use should be made of space with sufficient shelving to store all material.

These general requirements allow for considerable variation in layout and design. Whatever you end up with will have been considerably influenced by the machinery in your particular cutting room. Experience will demonstrate that the position of the machine is the most important variable to get right. Its relation to the sync bench is also very important if your method of working includes considerable moving to and fro between the synchronizer and the machine. There is no point in having a very neat room if the relationship between the various items in it is at variance to the way they are used.

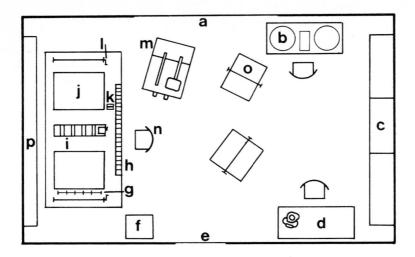

35 Cutting-room layout for Moviola and sync bench: *a* window with blinds; *b* rewind bench; *c* Dexion storage shelving for film cans; *d* desk; *e* door; *f* waste film bin; *g* horse; *h* sync bench; *i* synchronizer or picture synchronizer; *j* film bags; *k* tape joiner; *l* rewinds; *m* Moviola; *n* swivel chair; *o* trim bin; *p* shelf for film

The Moviola is placed to avoid light from the window. The room is divided into editor's space on the left and assistant's space on the right. If it can be afforded a flat-bed machine can replace the rewind bench to double as a viewing machine, and the assistant can also have a sync bench

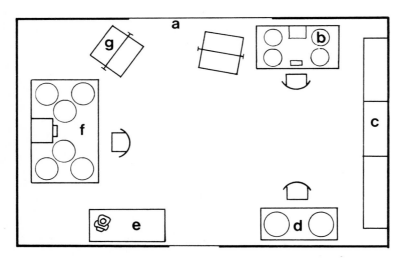

36 Cutting-room layout for flat-bed: *a* window with blinds; *b* 4-plate flat-bed; *c* shelving for film boxes; *d* rewind bench; *e* desk; *f* 6-plate flat-bed; *g* trim bin

This is typical of German cutting rooms where sync benches are virtually unknown. The assistant works at a 4-plate machine and the editor at a 6-plate

(In both diagrams relative dimensions are not meant to be accurate and the trim bins are of course moved to where required when working)

4 Cutting procedure

It should never be forgotten that film editing is a craft in which those involved have a tactile relationship with their 'material'. Although the 'material' is not shaped by the editor as clay is shaped by the potter, the way in which the editor relates physically to his footage will affect his sympathy and harmony with the process of shaping the cut film. I cannot stress this too strongly for those aiming to become editors or to edit their own material; watch any first-rate editor and it will not be long before you sense his relationship with film as a substance.

This basic tactile nature explains the logic of much about the way editors tend to work. Like good cooks, they prefer to have all their ingredients to hand – consequently the material must be organized and accessible. For some reason many people find the need for systems in a cutting room hard to accept. Actually, there is nothing obsessive or curious about it at all. Putting together a film is a complex process, and anyone successfully engaged in it will tell you that the greatest enemy, assuming good material, is anything that inhibits a positive work rhythm or stifles the development of momentum. I have known people so anxious to see a first cut of their material that they have ignored all advice to do the preparatory work, dived straight in, produced a cut in record time, and subsequently only avoided becoming suicidal when trying to re-cut by reprinting large amounts of material.

So the bulk of this chapter is about organizing the material to make it *most* accessible during the cutting process – a day spent preparing at this stage will save a week at a later stage of frustrating searches, resynchronization, re-transfers, reprinting and all such admissions of defeat which the editor cannot afford. One further point to bear in mind while reading this chapter: different kinds of film require different approaches in cutting. For instance, no one in his right mind would treat the footage for an observational documentary in the same way as the slates for a scripted drama.

CHECKING YOUR MATERIAL FOR FAULTS

No film should be looked at (after the mute viewing to check for camera, stock and laboratory faults) until the paperwork has been organized. If the film is fiction this written material may include camera sheets, sound reports, continuity notes, shot lists and marked-up script (see p. 40), all of which affect the way the footage is viewed and contain information about possible faults and sources of conflict which make choice of take and section of shot always a matter for compromise. For example, the best take for camera will not always be the best for sound and neither may be the one the director prefers for performance.

The laboratory rushes report is the other main source of information which will tell you if there are faults to be dealt with. However, as it does not always tell you everything about the state of the material, a proper viewing of mute rushes, on a projector, should be held *immediately* after processing, preferably attended by director, cameraman and editor to ensure nothing escapes unnoticed. This assumes that the editor is on the production during shooting, a luxury seldom possible except with feature films and the most elaborate of television programmes. (On most features the rushes are synchronized and viewed by lunchtime on the day after being shot, so the mute viewing is rendered redundant.) There are obvious advantages in having the editor on the pay-roll from the start of shooting, especially if he can achieve a rough cut of sequences very soon after they are processed. This gives the director and crew the chance to be sure they have obtained all the necessary material satisfactorily. The editor may well make useful suggestions for additional shots or re-shoots, and directors who have confidence in their editors will ring from location to ask specific questions about the effectiveness of material.

The following checklist should assist in the interpretation of remarks in the laboratory report and other paperwork and in dealing with faults discerned by yourself:

1   *Scratches*   Check if on print or in negative.
   (a)   *Positive*   Ensure that the projector and editing equipment are clean and properly aligned to avoid further damage (badly scratched cutting copy is a hindrance to good judgment in cutting).
   (b)   *Negative*   Check if they are emulsion or base scratches. Base scratches will usually polish out but emulsion scratches are a bigger problem and can be a reason to reject material. Also check if they are caused by camera or in processing and take remedial action.

2   *Dirt or 'sparkle'*   In general, positive dirt is black and negative white.
   (a)   *Positive*   Dirt on the print usually implies that equipment needs cleaning. A dirty cutting copy is as much a hindrance as a scratched one.
   (b)   *Negative*   If negative 'sparkle' is sufficiently worrying it is advisable to ask the laboratory to clean the negative and supply another rush print for checking. (N.B. It is unfortunately all too common to receive rushes which are dirty at the front and end of camera rolls on 16mm. With luck this will not spoil your irreplaceable shot that was snatched just before the film ran out.)
   (c)   *Hairs etc. in camera gate*   These usually appear at the top, bottom or side of frame. Check whether they are in the camera or projector by asking the projectionist to rack the picture to reveal the frame line.

3   *Fogging*   Head-, tail- and edge-fogging can all result from inefficient loading or from a badly fitting magazine. If the rush print is black-and-white the full extent of fogging will only be appreciated if a colour print is obtained.

4   *Static*   If your stock becomes electrically charged during exposure, patterns (known as 'Christmas trees' which they sometimes resemble), will appear on the processed material. There is no treatment for this, but it is sometimes caused by friction or rubbing in the camera, so the cameraman should be notified.

5   *Over- or under-exposure*   Since rush prints are almost invariably not

corrected for variations in exposure, there will normally be a degree of variation in density. However, if there is unacceptable heaviness or lightness in the print a check should be made of the negative and, if the laboratory thinks it is correctable, a graded print should be obtained. If there is a general trend away from the norm of exposure, checks should be made of the film stock and lens ratings (speeds) and efficiency of exposure meters.

6 *Soft focus*   Remember that differential focus and shots in which the focus is altered will probably be related to changes in the point of interest. The effectiveness of change of focus can consequently only be judged when material is synchronized. General out-of-focus rushes imply bad columnation of lenses, 'finger trouble' or just plain carelessness.

7 *Camera mechanism*   Your laboratory report may mention a number of faults which are due to irregularities in the camera:
    (a)   Intermittent exposure variations: 'flicker'.
    (b)   Irregularity of focus: 'breathing'.
    (c)   Unsteadiness of image: 'weaving' or 'floating'.

8 *Lens aberrations*   Various forms of image distortion can be caused by faults in the lenses. With careful and regular testing these problems are very rare.

9 *Stock faults ·*   There are several ways in which faulty stock can affect your material and you should always consider this a possible cause. The manufacturers admit the minimal liability of stock replacement if they accept responsibility.

10 *Processing*   Mistakes are also made in the laboratory and, prevention always being better than cure, you should ensure (a) that camera sheets are clearly written and special instructions always included where necessary, and (b) that you establish an immediate rapport with your 'contact' at the laboratory to whom any problems can then be referred personally (see p. 117).

11 *Extraneous objects*   Last but not least, boom shadows, microphones and cables in shot can easily be overlooked when viewing rushes for the first time.

SYNCHRONIZING THE RUSHES

Let us assume that all the rushes have been viewed and any necessary steps taken to rectify faults. The next task of the editing department is to see that the $\frac{1}{4}$-in. tapes are sent for transfer to magnetic film – they are almost always dealt with by a specialist sound facility, either in plant or elsewhere. If, however, you are able to do the transfer yourself then it is just a matter of gaining access to the facilities.

Assuming there is no bad news from the transfer you now proceed to synchronize your rushes. The most common form of sync marking is still the clapperboard but the basic method holds true for 'bleep' or 'blip' sync and even for the mike tap or hand clap (see p. 28). Nothing is either more important or more boring than this process – unless each and every take of every slate is synchronized to the exact frame you are storing up trouble for yourself when you embark on cutting. A synchronizer should always be used because it locks together picture and sound without any system of linkage that allows differential movement. Machines that are belt-driven or can be decoupled between the picture and sound transport encourage error in synchronization. Since 16mm sync is already relatively imprecise (35 mm, having 4 perforations to each frame, is much more accurate), anything which encourages this imprecision is to be avoided at all cost.

The advantage of a viewing machine with a larger screen than that available on a picture synchronizer is obvious. Even the most efficient crew is sometimes unable to provide in-focus, well-lit, large, steady clapperboards and so it may be necessary to run picture rushes for marking up on a Steenbeck or Moviola – essential if there is no sync reference. Some editors prefer always to mark up picture rushes by this method – it certainly has advantages and, with all due deference to camera assistants, provides an immediate and thorough check against the camera sheets. Also, laboratories often join camera rolls together out of order and, by running all picture rushes on the machine, rolls can be broken down and marked up in chronological slate order.

The following points take you step by step through the process of synchronization:

1   Place the roll of picture on the horse and insert in the synchronizer.
2   Find the first clapperboard and isolate the first frame which shows the board closed.
3   Mark up with white or yellow chinagraph, using the standard mark for picture sync, thus:

The horizontal lead-in line (extended over several frames) allows for quick identification when searching for sync at speed.

4   Remove picture from synchronizer, place the relevant sound roll on the horse and insert this in the synchronizer.
5   Locate the corresponding sound announcement and mark up the frame which contains the FRONT EDGE of the noise of the clapperboard closing, with the standard mark for sound sync, thus:

6   Reinsert the picture 'in synchronization' and write the slate and take numbers next to the lead-in line on both picture and track, e.g. ---------- × ----------13 – 2. (N.B. It is best not to use a diagonal line, e.g. 13/2, between slate and take since this can easily be mistaken for a 1; some editors even prefer 13T2 for total clarity.)
7   Always retain 2–3 feet in front of the sync frame to allow for lacing of each slate on an editing machine when you have broken down the film. This is more essential on a Steenbeck since a Moviola requires only a few frames to engage.
8   This being the front of the sync roll, join 20–30 feet of single perforation spacing to the front of this slate and add sync marks half way along both for ease of lacing when projected and for the coding machine.

9   Mark the front of each roll thus: 'TITLE', SYNC RUSHES, SLATES: X–Y, HEAD, ACTION OR SOUND. If white spacer is used it is possible to use colour coding to allow quick identification of picture and sound, e.g. black felt-tip pen for picture and red for sound.

10 The front of these rolls can now be attached to spools on the take-up arm and reeled down to the end of the marked-up slate.

11 Level sync should now be marked across the frame line. However, where either sound or picture continues beyond the other and is considered important enough to retain (if in doubt *always* retain material), then spacing must be inserted in the roll that has stopped first, until the other one finishes.

12 Either in level sync or after spacing has been added, both rolls can be guillotined and the next take put into sync and joined on to the tail of the previous one.

13 This process should be continued until you have about 1000 feet. Then add spacing to the tail with a level sync mark for checking.

14 Now remove this roll from the take-up arm and rewind it in sync, using the tail sync mark, for an immediate check of the complete roll.

15 These rolls of picture and sound should now be put into cans, clearly labelled with the same information as the front of the roll (see 9 above). The material is now ready for the coding machine.

Additional points to note in synchronizing rushes

1   Wild tracks are best removed from the sound material, rewound and identified before being put into a can for later use. It is a good idea to list the wild tracks in terms of purpose, approximate length and quality to avoid lengthy and often disappointing searches at the end of the cutting. *Never* assume because a wild track has been recorded to cover a scene or specific effect, that it is any more than a token effort on the part of the recordist to supply what he divines as necessary. The very fact that sync sound has not been recorded is often a good enough reason to suspect that wild tracks will not be usable. Therefore the list is only worthwhile if it is an accurate representation of what is usable. (Otherwise at midnight when you are laying tracks for mixing the following day you will realize too late that library sound should have been obtained to cover the scene in question.)

2   Mute picture should also be removed and identified, unless it is very short and directly related to the sync slates immediately adjacent, when it is best left in the sync roll and spacing added to the sound roll.

3   Both wild tracks and mute picture should be identified in chinagraph. Normally reference is made to the scene or slate to which they are relevant, thus: W/T after 13–2 and M after 13–2. Some mute of course is identified with the clapperboard. There are exceptions to this, e.g., wild track is sometimes recorded as general background and is then identified as W/T to cover scene X or slates X to Y. Occasionally a shot intended as sync lacks sound and will have to be post-recorded. In this case it can be labelled 13–2 No Sound, to differentiate it from a strictly mute shot.

4   If a take has been end-boarded then a simple sync mark and identification should be added near the front for lacing up when it is separated from the roll.

5   When using spacing in the sound roll, always ensure that the emulsion

side of the spacing is joined so that it faces the opposite way to the oxide of the magnetic track. Otherwise the emulsion will clog the sound heads and cause wear to the track itself.

6 There is no need to use the diagonal cutter for sound when synchronizing rushes as the cuts made at this stage will not be used in the final film. This helps to speed the process and makes for easier handling when the film is broken down.

7 *Never* assume that because the clapperboard is in sync, the whole take remains in sync. A faulty lead or a low battery can cause loss of sync in recording and mistakes can be made in transfer. Therefore always make spot-checks, taking advantage of any natural substitute for a clapperboard, such as door slams or – the best alternative – words beginning with a B or P. If a take is found to be out of sync it is best to confirm *all* the slates on that tape roll since the checks necessary when reloading the tape recorder may not have been done properly. You can then explore the possibility of whether a transfer can be made to adjust the sync. If this is out of the question you should determine whether sound or picture is longer and by how much. If sound is slightly longer (say by a frame per foot), it is possible to remove the excess frames at regular intervals. If either is *a great deal* longer it is probably best to consider post-synchronization or, in the last resort, to reject the material. If picture is slightly longer you have a trickier situation. Obviously, removing frames from the picture will not work as, when the negative is cut to match, the ensuing print will jump; and adding frames to the sound is awkward,

37 A Moy numbering machine, the traditional device which uses ink to mark the film

38 An Acmade numbering machine which marks film by using a coloured tape to transfer the numbers from the block to the film surface

especially with distinctive background on the track. It is possible to stretch or concertina the sound whilst retaining the pitch of the original, but this is an expensive process and only to be recommended if the track is irreplaceable and essential.

8   Never treat sound (at this or any other stage) as the element you are adding to the picture. The best marriage of the two is a total synthesis, so you must apply the same sort of quality checks to your sound that I outlined for picture during the mute viewing. One factor that reduces the respect accorded to sound is that, except in feature films, the sound you synchronize to the picture cutting copy is the same that is used to re-record from when mixing, whereas the cutting copy is a mere work print. (In feature films no one would normally dare to take the mutilated, worn-out, working track to the dubbing theatre; indeed the higher status accorded the sound track in feature films is recognized by there being a separate sound editor.)

CODING THE RUSHES

Once all material has been synchronized, or as each roll is rewound and checked, it is ready for coding or numbering. Except in large studios it is unusual for cutting rooms to have access to their own coding machine, so it is normal to use a firm that provides a numbering service.

The coding machine indelibly marks your picture and sound material at 1-foot intervals along the edge, with numbers which progress automatically by one digit at a time. On 16mm the numbering block usually has 6 digits which consist of 2 letters and 4 numbers, or 6 numbers. So your first roll of picture and sound can be numbered AA0000–AA1000 or 01 0000–01 1000, the second AB or 02 and so on. It is worth noting that with an 8-digit block it becomes possible to code using the appropriate slate and take, e.g. slate 243 take 7 becomes 24370000 onwards.

All professional editors prefer to work with coded material. It has the following advantages:

1   The alternative for logging purposes is to use key numbers. Coding is preferable because:
   (a)   Key numbers are often indistinct in the rush print.
   (b)   Coding supplies you with the same reference for picture and sound.
2   It provides a level sync mark every foot.
3   Trims can be easily located.

I am convinced that the slight delay involved before cutting can commence is a small price to pay for the value of coding your material.

LOGGING

The nature of the log that you must now make of your material will be determined by several factors, the most important of which are (a) the kind of film you are working on and (b) what other paperwork already exists as reference for the editor. On a scripted drama, where shot lists, camera and sound reports, continuity notes and a marked-up script are also available, the log may only need to consist of slate and take numbers, and the corresponding head and tail code numbers. However, on documentary much more information is usually added, including descriptions and quality of each shot. Illustrated here is a simple form of log sheet. Remember that the prime purpose of your log is to enable you to find material from a simple number reference.

TRANSCRIBING OR MARKING UP THE SCRIPT

The next step depends entirely on whether your film is documentary or fiction. With documentary, it is best now carefully to transcribe all interview or conversational material, with slate reference, as a shorthand guide to cutting. However, never treat the transcription as a substitute for cutting the film itself, because the words on paper cannot convey voice inflexion or the rhythm. So it is best to use the transcription in conjunction with viewing the material. With fiction, it is the practice of some editors at this stage to mark up the script. If continuity notes have been provided, this is a simple process of representing the coverage for each scene on the relevant page of the script. However, there are refinements to this system. One is to wait until the synchronized rushes have been seen with the director, and only to mark up the script with those takes that are chosen to be used rather than all that have been printed. Another is to obtain polythene sleeves for the script pages, so that the marking up can be done in chinagraph on the sleeve and altered when decisions are made, thus representing the cut film in a graphic form. This will be a very useful cross-reference (and will protect the script from the otherwise inevitable deterioration). See ill. 20.

VIEWING THE SYNC RUSHES

Everything described so far should have happened before the viewing of sync rushes, unless they are being viewed daily as shooting progresses. This viewing is important not least for the relationship and understanding

THE NATIONAL FILM SCHOOL BEACONSFIELD			RUSHES LOG				

DATE 6 · 3 · 81   TITLE ' *HIATUS* '

ROLL No	SLATE No - Tk	SCENE No	RUBBER NUMBERS		MUTE OR SYNC	DESCRIPTION	OK / NG
			FROM	TO			
1	1 — 1	5	AA0000	0012	S	C·U· JOHN - (LINES WRONG)	N/G
	1 - 2	5	0013	0025	S	" "	OK
	2 — 1	5	0026	0031	M	C·U· DAVID REACTION	
	3 - 1	5	0032	0040	S	TWO-SHOT JOHN/DAVID (Mike in shot)	N/G
	3 - 2	5	0041	0049	S	" " —	OK
	3 - 3	5	0050	0057	S	" " "	OK
	4 - 1	17	0058	0066	M	C·U· PHONE	OK
	5 - 1	17	0067	0093	M	C·U· PHONE (ALTERNATIVE ANGLE)	OK
	6 - 1	17	0094	0134	S	WIDE-SHOT FIGHT (CAMERA FAULT)	N/G
	6 - 2	17	0135	0176	S	" " " (LAMP KNOCKED OVER)	N/G
	6 - 3	17	0177	0238	S	" " "	OK
	6 - 4	17	0239	0280	S	" " "	OK
	6 - 5	17	0281	0324	S	" " "	OK
	7 - 1	17	0325	0337	S	B·C·U· HANDS ON THROAT	OK
	7 - 2	17	0338	0349	S	" " " "	OK
	8 - 1	17	0350	0371	M	C·U· REVERSE ANGLE	OK
	9 - 1	17	0372	0385	M	WIDE SHOT DAVID RELEASES JOHN & STANDS UP	OK

39 This log sheet does not include key numbers since editors usually refer to the rubber (code) numbers. Key numbers are more important when relating the print to the negative or original

between director and editor (see p. 73). But you should not expect too many concrete decisions to be reached at this stage: it is much more important to get a feel of the material and to begin to relate the script as written to the film as realized. There are many editors who find it impossible to imagine the 'look' of a film even from the most lucid scenario, but this is not necessarily a disadvantage since the particular vision a director brings to a film will invariably not mesh with the perceptions of others. Indeed, if the editor has too clear an idea of how the film should look he stands the chance of being very disappointed at rushes. If director and editor are one and the same person, this is the time when you come face to face with the reality of your material. There is no way that the experience of shooting the film can be wiped from your memory, but the more you can treat what you see on the screen in the viewing theatre as the reality, and forget any imagined ideal realization of the script, the easier it will be to make the most of editing's contribution to the final result.

If possible the material should be assembled in scene order for this screening, to give an immediate sense of the whole material for each scene and of the way scenes may or may not be constructed to flow together. New and exciting juxtapositions may emerge later but the ideas that can transform a cut that is slave to the script are always more likely to emerge if the editor has digested the expected form first.

At this viewing it is very useful to make notes of particular reactions you have to the material aside from the indications given you in the paperwork (see p. 40) supplied from various members of the crew. You should now begin to feel the possible shape of sequences. Remember that one element in a few seconds of an otherwise poor take may make it the best alternative for that moment in the film. It is too easy to fall into the trap of looking for the perfect combination of these elements, when there is advantage to be had from choosing a nuance of performance in a take that is less good than others for lighting, operation, sound and overall rhythm. Judging which elements are more important than the rest is also part of this effort to familiarize yourself with the footage. It will not all happen at once, and first impressions, right or wrong, are often superficial: the relevance of a shot may only be revealed as the overall structure takes shape during cutting.

Even if little seems to sink in as a result of projecting your synchronized rushes, it is always a better approach than plunging straight into cutting without a clear map of the outline of the material in your mind. Of course, if you are cutting fiction, you have a map in the shape of a shooting script but even attempting to cut to that script may lead you up blind alleys which you can avoid if the viewing is held first.

BREAKING DOWN THE FILM

After screening, the footage is broken down for ease of working. Several factors may affect the system employed. Let us take the example of a scripted fiction film first. Assuming that a reasonably clear idea has emerged of which takes are to be employed in the cut, each of these chosen takes is broken out of its sync roll and rewound, on 16mm usually with both picture and sound on the same core, and clearly labelled. If possible all the slates for a particular scene should be put in the same can. The takes remaining on the roll are canned separately and labelled as 'spares' for the appropriate scene or scenes. This system is ideal for editing with a synchronizer and Moviola or with a motorized picture-sychronizer. It can also be employed when using a table editing-machine, but in that case the first cut working from broken-down rushes is inevitably more laborious and less fluid (see comments on use of different machinery, p. 52). The machine you are using may affect how you decide to file the material.

Documentary footage is seldom broken down into single shots unless those shots are inordinately long. The guideline here is to leave the subject material in rolls that make sense of it but that are not too long to prevent relatively swift reference to any particular shot. In any case 16mm rolls of more than 400 feet (10 minutes) are very cumbersome when you are searching for a few frames – which invariably turn out to be at the far end of the roll!

It should be mentioned here that sometimes the dialogue will be post-synchronized before cutting. This is usually because there is a greater chance of the artist being available at this early stage. Post-synchronization is discussed in detail in Chapter 6.

CUTTING

Once all the material has been broken down and filed you can proceed with the cutting of the first sequence. Unless there are specific reasons to do otherwise, such as the need to cut a sequence early for post-synchronization, always start at the beginning. This may seem obvious, but it is sometimes very tempting to begin with a particularly vivid scene or one that has struck you as attractive when reading the script. In documentary there is sometimes no way of knowing what is the beginning, in which case devise some guideline to give you a sense of overall structure to allow the first cut to emerge: chronology is the most obvious yardstick but there may be others.

The next chapter deals in detail with attitudes to and reasons for cutting. Remember that in all cases where you as editor are expected to make a substantial contribution to the form of the final film the way you approach each stage of the cut will inevitably affect your perception of the structure. It is always better if you end up revealing an essentially innate form rather than seeking to impose an artificial shape.

To begin cutting arrange all the material for the sequence on the bench in front of you, in the order you expect to use the shots, using the marked-up script as reference. At this point I am unable to avoid what to many editors is a heresy. The widely accepted procedure is to construct an assembly from which a rough cut and eventually a fine cut are produced. It has always seemed to me to be counter-productive to insert extra stages in the process, when the only way that you can tell whether each sequence is working is to cut it properly. The assembly seems to me to be a way of reducing editing to the level of 'painting by numbers'. It makes the framework predetermined and allows less flexibility later. Whereas, even if it does not work first time, an attempt at a real cut gives you information that can be applied to a re-cut. More than that: as the cut comes together the cumulative effect of each cut and each scene on the rest will emerge dynamically. Editing has to be a process of cause and effect, of the synthesis created from juxtapositions. The first few cuts when jumping in the deep end are always hard, not to say traumatic, but there is nothing worse than the limp structure that results from nibbling away rather than tackling the task head-on.

Of course, there are sequences that can only be constructed little by little but, even if you are presented with two or three rolls of material that are supposed to be magically transformed into a dazzling montage, always look for the core idea. If the sequence is worth having it must have a point in the film. Finding that purpose and applying it to the evaluation of each shot will always give you more of a basis for constructing a sequence than the principle of 'stick it together and see how it goes'. Sometimes the criterion is as simple as direction of movement within the shots, or some form of progression that allows the film to flow from one scene to the next.

Whatever approach to cutting you come to favour, a positive attitude is essential. No procedure should be applied for its own sake, but only because you believe that by the method you employ you stand the best chance of making the most of the material.

The actual process of cutting with a tape joiner has been described (see p. 55). Some of the cuts you make will not remain the same, so the most important part of organizing the way you edit is to ensure that the material remains as accessible as possible. Remember that the trim bin is no substitute for a proper filing system (see p. 57). It is also best to rejoin head and tail trims of each shot so that they can be easily re-run when considering alterations. If this is not done you will begin to experience the worst aspect of disorganization in the cutting room. As each cut is made the trims become a separate collection of pieces so that towards the end of the process you find that every time a few frames are required there are three or four places to look: the original can, the trim bins and various cans marked 'assembly trims' or 'fourth fine cut trims'! The exasperation this produces can be soul-destroying, and the refinement that is invariably necessary to arrive at a fine cut worth the name may be seriously jeopardized.

For consistency it is as well to apply the following marks during cutting:

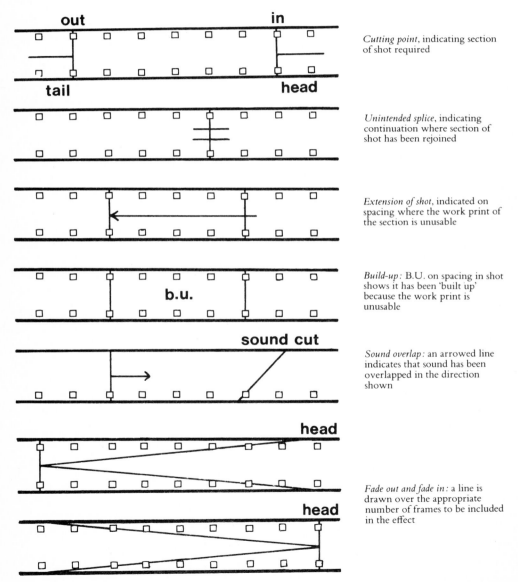

Cutting point, indicating section of shot required

Unintended splice, indicating continuation where section of shot has been rejoined

Extension of shot, indicated on spacing where the work print of the section is unusable

Build-up: B.U. on spacing in shot shows it has been 'built up' because the work print is unusable

Sound overlap: an arrowed line indicates that sound has been overlapped in the direction shown

Fade out and fade in: a line is drawn over the appropriate number of frames to be included in the effect

40 Standard markings used during cutting

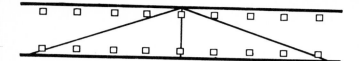

Dissolve or mix: a line is drawn each side of the cut point over the number of frames to be included in the effect

THE RELATIONSHIP BETWEEN DIRECTOR AND EDITOR

One indication of the importance of the relationship between directors and their editors is that frequently the same editor will work with a director on a number of his films. It has even been known for directors to alter their schedule to fit in with the availability of their favourite editor. There are many cases of consistent and continuing collaboration between directors and editors: Chabrol has used Jacques Gaillard for the majority of his films; Bresson has consistently worked with Raymond Lamy; Reginald Mills and then Reginald Beck have shared almost all the editing credits on Losey's films; and Dede Allen has cut many of the films made by Sidney Lumet and Arthur Penn.

The relationship will vary enormously in each case. Some directors merely require a good and reliable technician, others expect and depend upon a much more creative contribution. There is also considerable variation in working methods. Most editors do not like to have the directors breathing down their necks all the time; by far the most effective way is to meet regularly, say for an hour each day, and to discuss what has been cut since the last meeting and to review the material for the next sequence or sequences due to be cut. Of course, the nature of the material will affect how often and for how long consultations need to take place, but only where director and editor are completely relaxed and in tune with each other will it be possible to work together constantly without considerable tension developing.

It is not enough just to be sympathetic in attitude to your director. To make the most positive contribution an editor should take the following steps:

1 Read the script *in advance of* cutting.
2 Become familiar with the director's previous work.
3 Read any background material relevant to the film.
4 Meet the cameraman, sound recordist and other major contributors to the film who might affect your own job.
5 Liaise with the continuity or production assistant for documentation.
6 Make yourself known to the laboratory contact.
7 Choose your assistant carefully for both efficiency and tact.
8 Find out your director's preferred working hours and eating habits!
9 Ensure that the cutting room is properly set up *before* cutting starts.
10 Make sure that reliable maintenance can be obtained for your equipment.

If you think any of the above is unnecessary then you should not be an editor. It is easy enough to be a good technician, but the satisfaction to be gained from editing is in direct proportion to the effort you make to demonstrate a real commitment.

5 The language of editing: giving your material form and refining its meaning

In *The Parade's Gone By* Brownlow wrote: 'Editing is directing the film for the second time. To gauge the psychological moment – to know exactly where to cut – requires the same intuitive skill as that needed by a director.' Every film presents the editor with an imprecise agenda. Without experience it is natural to conclude that a well-cut film only requires the editor to put the pieces together in the right order. In fact, no editor believes that his task is simply to find the one perfect conjuction that is just waiting to be discovered. If this were so cutting would be analogous to jigsaw solving.

The difference between editing a film and assembling a jigsaw is that with a film nothing is completely predetermined. The film-maker may claim that the film already exists in his head, and that it is also on paper in the script, but the film that emerges from the cutting room has never existed before, neither in someone's head nor on paper. It is only through the editing process that the material is translated into the form that can communicate its narrative and meaning to the audience.

To understand the language of editing requires us to define in what ways it involves 'directing the film for the second time'. In that way we can unearth what Brownlow calls 'the hidden power' of the editor.

Selection
The way films are conceived and shot assumes the function of editing. This is especially true in the selection of what is to be shot, a process that leaves levels of decision-making to be refined in the cutting. In dramatic films this provides the editor with different kinds of choices. The first is the choice between several attempts at the same shot. Every time two or more takes are shot on the same slate selection in the editing is being allowed for. This implies both the desire to obtain the most effective version of the action for a particular shot and the realization that the choice of take may depend on which one dovetails best into other shots which cover the same segment of the script. Secondly, it is normal to shoot the same action in more than one set-up: the resulting changes of angle and sizes of shot allow a further level of selection in the cutting. Thirdly, this kind of shooting leaves open the question of when to cut and what to cut to.

Structuring
To be able to understand the way in which editing selects, you must first understand the structuring of a scene and also the placing of each scene in the overall film. To be able to structure a scene effectively you must understand its function. It is the misunderstanding of function that leads to the most superficial use of editing technique. If the writing and/or

shooting of a film is meant to convey more than just the words and actions of its characters then the cutting must be used to serve those aspects of the drama that lie beneath the surface. If you edit merely to ensure that the dialogue is heard and the actions seen then your structuring will be only something mechanical.

Helen van Dongen arrived at her own list of factors affecting the structuring of material through her experience as Flaherty's editor: the subject-matter of the scene; spatial movement in each image; the tonal value of each shot (atmosphere); the emotional content. This can be taken to represent the specific agenda for documentaries, although in general terms it overlaps in its application to dramatic material.

Balance and emphasis
The real contribution of editing is to provide support to the inherent drama through balance and emphasis. The balance in a scene is a delicate matter which must be retained with every cut, and if we use emphasis correctly it will help this balance. For instance, each time you cut to a closer shot it is imperative that the shift in visual emphasis supports the dramatic balance at that point.

The dynamic axis
Already in the way a scene is staged – in the way character and camera movement are controlled – the director is seeking to use physical space to support the emotional content of the scene by balance and emphasis. Editing should respect and reinforce these intentions. As each scene evolves the editor must be aware of changes in the dominant line of dramatic tension, or what I like to call the dynamic axis. This is not simply a matter of analysing the flow of a scene and deciding who is 'centre stage' at any point; any such obvious dominance must be taken in conjunction with the point of the scene and its purpose in the overall drama. To take a simple example, if a fight occurs between two characters it may be that the effect on a third party not directly involved in the fight is more important in the film than the actual conflict. The reactions of this third party could be the element that the cutting needs to emphasize. Even here, you have to be careful not to over-emphasize by cutting: for instance, the director may have carefully staged the action to focus on reactions of the third party while still including the other two characters in the shot. Understanding this dynamic axis in a scene will always give the editor the right clues in deciding what to cut to and when.

Motivation
All cuts should be motivated. Again it must be emphasized that this is not something mechanical. Just because there is movement that could be followed or emphasized by a cut is not necessarily enough reason for the cut. The dramatic focus of a scene and the point of view that has been established are often far more important than the details of the action. Staying wide can sometimes serve the tension far better than cutting in close, and the cut to a close-up may provide undue emphasis on the insignificant.

Point of focus
The editor must be aware that at each moment in a shot the audience's attention is focused on a particular area of the frame. Often a cut that is

sufficiently motivated is prevented from working properly by the switch of attention on the cut. If the eye has to adjust its focus in an unexpected way the moment of the cut will be a dead spot and will dislocate the flow of the scene.

Sequencing

We must also be aware of the way in which cuts work at the junctions between scenes. Much will depend upon the way the director has ensured that the shots that are meant to open and close each adjacent scene can be matched in the cutting. The success of sequencing will be affected by the composition and, of course, by the control of pace and rhythm.

Parallel action

Scenes that are meant to be cut in parallel are often conceived without due attention being given to the pacing and balance. Such intercutting will seldom work unless the material has been preconceived for that purpose, especially since the normal function of parallel action is to lead to a denouement which brings together the separate dramatic threads.

Rhythm and pacing

As we construct a scene the aim must be to provide the right pacing and to establish or emphasize the inherent rhythm. In both dramatic and documentary films the events being shown have a natural rhythm. It is important to be able to use this rhythm to motivate the cutting. Of all the elements which must be considered for effective use of the editing process, the use of and control of rhythm and pace are finally what will determine the contribution that cutting makes to your film.

Kurosawa had in mind a particular piece of music when conceiving one sequence of *Red Beard* (1964). According to Donald Ritchie in *The Films of Akira Kurosawa* (1965), when Kurosawa had cut the sequence together, he 'put on a recording of the Haydn, the second movement, and played it along with the film to see what the effect was. Well, the effect was just fine, but what really surprised me was that I had cut the sequence so that it came to an end precisely at the end of the Haydn. . . Somewhere in the back of my head some kind of clock kept count.' Of course, the material had the potential to work effectively but it was the editing that confirmed the inherent rhythm and pace.

In his article, *Montage mon beau souci* (1956), Godard stated: 'If direction is a look, montage is a heartbeat. To foresee is the characteristic of both, but what one seeks to foresee in space the other seeks in time.' When he wrote this Godard had only made two short films, but foreseeing in time is indeed the prime function of editing. Everything we do in cutting is in some sense a manipulation of time. We speed it up, slow it down, repeat it, truncate it, stop it, go forwards and backwards in it, and remove the need for it to get us from one place to another or indeed from one camera set-up to another. We even combine the same time in more than one place by parallel cutting. We use our perceptions of time to cheat time.

Ultimately it is our ability to control the rhythm and pace in cutting that makes it possible to play with time in this way, but because we have this power as editors it is also possible to lose control. For no shot is neutral, both its content and its form already contain the elements which contribute to the innate rhythm that reacts upon any juxtaposition we create. If you make one significant change in a sequence, even if it seems to be well cut, the result will always have a rippling effect on the feeling of the rest of the sequence, and it is unlikely that you will get away with making just that one adjustment.

REASONS FOR CUTTING

Cutting is always a matter of balance and emphasis, a delicate structuring of elements, and while a cut is never right or wrong in an absolute sense, we can say it works or does not work in relation to the rest of a sequence. Unfortunately it is a common error in cutting to rationalize the logic of particular cuts without due reference to their place in a sequence. If you watch a good editor at work you will notice the way he backs up a considerable number of feet before running the film to check a change he has made. This procedure springs from an awareness that the cut is not simply a matter of what happens at the junction of two shots. That junction may be a perfect match of an action that continues across the cut, but the effect can still be wrong. This structural balance is not like strict tempo music. In fact, every cut involves a series of decisions which, with experience, become a subconscious checklist.

Positive reasons: analysing the elements of dramatic development
The most important thing is that your decision to cut should be based on positive reasons. An awareness of the general factors just discussed – structuring, balance and emphasis, the dynamic axis, rhythm and pacing, etc. – is the essential starting point. But it is only by then analysing the elements of dramatic development in the scene under consideration that you will be able to arrive at the correct *particular* solutions.

In attempting to respect dramatic development in cutting you should be aware of the following elements:

1   Is the audience to *identify* with a particular character or are we merely observers?
2   Does a particular character *dominate*; does that dominance shift during the scene?
3   Does the dialogue function as narrative or is it mere embroidery, i.e. aside from the real drama of the scene?
4   Is there a necessary eloquence in the silences?
5   How does the movement of camera and/or characters contribute to the scene?
6   Should the scene be carried wide or are close shots essential?
7   If we cut in close will it preclude cutting wide again?
8   Are there significant details that must be seen?
9   Does a reaction need to be explained?
10   Does a moment in the scene demand a shock cut to point up the drama?
11   Does the scene have a natural climax?
12   What elements apart from the characters are important to the scene?
13   Do other sounds have significance apart from the dialogue? and of course:
14   What is the function of the scene?
15   How does the scene fit into the overall film?

If you can answer these questions at each point that a cut seems appropriate, it will help to determine what to cut to and when. I am not claiming that during the process of editing these questions are consciously confronted, but they should be part of the unspoken agenda behind the way each sequence is structured.

Overcoming problems by cutting
Although the hundred and one bad reasons for cutting do not teach us positive lessons about editing, the remedies for such shortcomings can produce positive results:

1 *Uneven performance* The best delivery and characterization is sometimes spread in sections over more than one take. This can be improved by inserting reaction shots or by cutting to a different angle so that the best parts can each be used.

2 *Fluffs* If a word or short phrase contains a 'fluff' or wrong emphasis in an otherwise reasonable take it is often possible to replace the offending sound with the same words from another take or shot covering the same dialogue.

3 *Lack of reaction* Where a facial expression is 'dead' or the reaction shot does not even exist, look elsewhere in the scene for similar reactions which may not be needed in their proper place. It may even be possible to snatch the required few seconds from before the clapperboard or after the director shouts 'Cut'. This is one good reason for retaining all properly framed and exposed picture when synching up.

4 *Mismatched action* Sometimes an action cut that is essential will not work either because the change of angle is strange or because of considerable discrepancy in pace. In this case try cutting before the action or, if the sequence depends on rhythm for its effectiveness, you can sometimes use the movement of another character to match that in the outgoing shot. Indeed, it is always too easy to fall into the trap of trying to make a direct cut work when the best answer is to insert an alternative that does not depend on matching action or pace.

5 *Discrepancies in pacing* You must remain aware of whether the overall pace suits the mood of a scene. Where it seems too slow it may be necessary to overlap the dialogue or intercut more. Where the pace is too fast make use of the silences by inserting pauses contained in complementary shots.

6 *Unconvincing action* If action is unconvincing when cut together, the reactions of a third party with sound laid over often compensates (e.g. with a badly staged or performed fight scene). This does assume, of course, that the director has had the foresight to shoot such reactions.

7 *Lack of static before or after movement* Tracks and pans occasionally lack a satisfactory hold on the beginning or the end. Mixing from or to a relevant static shot can be an effective substitute or even improve the structure of the scene. Given even pace it is also effective to mix one movement into another, although this is hard when the movement continues in the same direction. A track or pan mixing to a zoom can often provide dramatic concentration.

8 *Problems of matching sound and picture* In dialogue scenes the best cutting point is often not available without offsetting the junction on the sound track. Firstly, what seems to be the best place in the dialogue may

not provide a convincing picture cut. In this case there are two solutions. You can either overlap the dialogue if this is appropriate to the mood of the scene, so that a good visual cut is created, or it may be possible to remove a phrase from the dialogue to achieve a similar result.

Secondly, where the dialogue already overlaps it may be necessary to continue the track from one of the two shots over the cut to retain the sense of the dialogue and still achieve an effective picture cut.

Other unsatisfactory juxtapositions can be improved by making use of hard sounds, such as door slams or gun shots, to bridge or signal the cut.

9 *Unconvincing dialogue* The scripted words are never sacrosanct and it is important to remain aware that dramatic flow can often be helped by removing phrases or even whole sentences. Again this is facilitated by inserting a reaction or just ending a scene sooner.

10 *Junctions between scenes* These are perhaps the most vital cutting points: always be prepared to acknowledge that a scene is overstaying its welcome or that it can start later. Once a scene has served its purpose it is criminal to hold on to it. However, the very essence of a particular sequence can be contained in the pause at the end, and in any case remember that the initial impact of each subsequent scene is dynamically affected by the *last moments* of the scene that precedes it.

CUTTING AND REACTION: DRAMATIC EMPHASIS

The psychology of film language is constantly being modified by the interactions between film-makers and the audience. Consider, for instance, the reaction shot. Reaction is perhaps the most basic tool of dramatic construction, without which all narrative lacks its essential driving force. Once movies had confirmed the validity of showing someone reacting to the words or actions of others, it seemed only natural to *cut* to that reaction. But once this possibility had been established film-makers soon became aware that cutting to the reaction was not necessarily the only way of dealing with the expectation provoked in the audience. In film the cut is now only one way of using this device. Staging can incorporate the reaction in several ways:

1 The camera can pan to the reaction.
2 The camera can track or zoom in or out to include the reaction.
3 Focus can be changed to emphasize the reaction.
4 The protagonist can turn or move in shot to include or reveal the reaction.
5 The person reacting can turn or move into shot for the reaction.
6 The reaction can be given in dialogue out of the shot, while the camera remains on the protagonist.
7 Conversely the build-up to the reaction can all be taken on the character from whom that reaction is expected.
8 The provocation and reaction can be represented by the way a 'neutral' observer responds to the whole interaction.

Most of these alternatives apply equally to both fiction and documentary filming, the only difference being that whereas in scripted films the *director* can choose in advance, in documentary the decision has to be made by the director and/or cameraman at the moment of shooting. The important point is that the cut is not the only way to deal with a shift in dramatic emphasis. However, more often than not the cover for a scene will still leave some choices available to the editor. For instance, a pan that reveals a reaction in wide shot can still lead to the feeling that a subsequent cut to close-up is justified. Indeed, the pan may alternatively give you the opportunity to cut back to the person who has provoked the reaction.

DIRECTORS AND EDITING – SOME EXAMPLES

There is great variance in the degree to which selection, structuring, pacing and rhythm are left to the cutting stage. Even in the same film a director may decide that some scenes are best structured in the way they are staged and that others are best handled in the cutting room.

The following examples are meant as a stimulus to the study of particular films. The choice is personal and obviously cannot be comprehensive.

KUROSAWA *Rashomon* (1950)

When we first meet the woodman the most important shot is one where the camera tracks alongside him as he runs through the forest. To begin with the camera is at some distance; but eventually it crosses his path in front of him in close-up and continues tracking, having reversed our point of view. Thus one shot has contained the man and his natural habitat from different perspectives and also conveyed a sense of movement. It is difficult to imagine a cut sequence that would have been as effective.

Later the bandit is sitting under a tree, beside a path through the forest. Eventually we see the woman being led past the spot on a horse by her

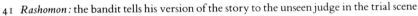

41 *Rashomon*: the bandit tells his version of the story to the unseen judge in the trial scene

husband. To increase the tension, Kurosawa intercuts several times between the bandit and his point of view and each time cheats the movement so that the progression is elongated (i.e. if you were to cut together the shots of the travellers the action would overlap at each cut). In this case if Kurosawa had contained the action in a wide shot the tension would have depended on real time and the spatial relationship between the characters. Also in *Rashomon*, as in many of his films, Kurosawa makes use of the American Cut: a cut in on the same angle for dramatic emphasis. In less sure hands this would merely appear clumsy but by controlling the *rhythm* he is able to defy the convention of change of angle.

One further aspect of *Rashomon* should be noted. The proceedings of the court are *always* seen from the point of view of the magistrate, who is *never* seen, only heard. This gives the court scenes an unremitting intensity and forces the audience to act as judge. The director sacrifices the possibility of controlling pace in the cutting because he is concerned with other aspects of dramatic emphasis. The camera is the magistrate, therefore the axis of the scene is the line between each member of the audience and the prisoner or witness being interrogated. Any change of angle or cut would have destroyed this line. The value of Kurosawa in examples like these is that he prevents us from considering that the conventional answer is necessarily the only one. Most of his films are similarly rewarding in the details of his technique.

BERGMAN *Persona* (1966)

In an interview with Peter Cowie in 1969 Bergman stated: 'Film is concerned above all with rhythm. . . . The primary factor is the image, the secondary factor is the sound, the dialogue; and the tension between these two creates the third dimension.'

In *Persona* Bergman is at times as audacious as Kurosawa in denying the conventional approach to editing. Through a narrative that has as a central dramatic element the wilful silence of one of the two main characters, he is able to construct sequences that emphasize the inaction and silence of this character through the restlessness and verbosity of the other. The watershed of the film and of the relationship between the two characters comes when Alma (the nurse) recounts her interpretation of Elisabet's (the silent patient) attitude to having a child. Firstly the statement is made while we watch Elisabet's face and *then* it is repeated whilst the camera is on Alma. At the end of this repetition the two faces merge in one image as if one or other of the two women has taken on the 'persona' of both.

Conventionally we would have expected an intercut sequence, building to a climax through the editing, but the impact that Bergman achieves makes us consider the implications *behind* the statement rather than the superficial effect on the characters. This is not a technique that can be easily applied to other situations in films, but it does point to a more general problem. The close-up is the most telling weapon in the armoury of cinema, but it has one particular disadvantage. In scenes between two characters there are invariably moments in the cutting when you feel torn between the alternatives of seeing either one or the other. Seeing both is a compromise that may not have the advantage of either. Constant intercutting can call attention to the technique.

42 *Persona*: the nurse and the patient, locked in a mental struggle for their own and each other's identity

Bergman's answer is really only an extension of the way all editing plays with time, and it is paid off by the masterly merging of the faces.

BUÑUEL *The Discreet Charm of the Bourgeoisie* (1972) and *Phantom of the Liberty* (1974)

In a conversation with Marianne Kärré, Bergman remarked: 'Have I borrowed anything in *Persona*? But of course, why wouldn't I borrow? Buñuel was my first cinematic revelation. He remained the most important for me . . . I entirely share his theory of initial shock to attract the public's attention.'

Buñuel's influence is most keenly felt in the opening montage of *Persona* which is climaxed by the jamming of the film in the projector and the image burning out. But his relevance to the contemporary film-maker is not limited to the anarchic, surreal elements that persist from his early attempts at cinema. For Buñuel, perhaps more than any other director, turns the use of the basic grammar of film into magic and mystery.

In relatively recent work such as *The Discreet Charm of the Bourgeoisie* and *Phantom of the Liberty* he effectively takes the linear nature of cinematic expression and resists the audience's desire for a continuously coherent narrative. By providing coincidental, accidental and providential connections between people and situations he uses conventional techniques to carry us along so that, instead of expecting and looking for a story, we become concerned with what Buñuel has to say about situations and attitudes.

In *Discreet Charm* dreams become reality, or do they? And the film is punctuated by the main characters walking along a flat uninteresting road as if Buñuel is saying: if you want narrative progression, this is all you are going to get. In *Phantom of the Liberty*, after the nurse has spent a bizarre and surreal night at the inn on her journey to Argenton, the film cuts to an older man having breakfast in the foreground as she comes down to pay the bill and leave. The man asks for a lift in her car and, without an elaborate cut sequence, they leave together and we find that when she drops him off, it is *his* story that we next follow. Our curiosity is aroused without any indulgence in fancy devices and the world within the film has its own irrefutable coherence. Each cut or substitute for it within the shot has superficial logic but the drama and Buñuel's comment on it are working continuously on other levels. This 'thrower of bombs', as Henry Miller called him in the 1930s, is a magician with a difference: he is more likely to produce hats out of rabbits than vice versa and to do it in such a way that the audience accepts it in terms other than those of logic. We all now can recognize and reject the library shot of the ferocious lion when it is intercut with the intrepid hero standing his ground, but when in *Phantom of the Liberty* the husband wakes up and sees animals and birds stalking about at the end of the bed we accept it because Buñuel has established his own *un*logic.

Since the hypocrisy of bourgeois, social, political and religious morality is his main target, the nonsensical becomes frighteningly rational. A study of Buñuel's editing, especially in these films, will confirm the way he uses conventional expectation in cutting, as well as in staging, to serve his own purposes.

BRESSON *Une Femme Douce* (1969)
Buñuel's characters are vivid and his situations extraordinary, a stark contrast to the cool, detached, ascetic approach of Bresson. He, like Bergman, is convinced that rhythm is the omnipotent aspect of cinematic language: 'Nothing is durable but what is caught up in rhythms. Bend context to form and sense to rhythms.' His object is 'to translate the invisible wind by the water it sculpts in passing'.

In his best films Bresson practises what he preaches with compelling success. Take the opening of *Une Femme Douce*. We start on a door handle, which seems to be held almost too long – an elderly woman opens the door – stands in the doorway – moves. The subjective camera sees a french window open on to a balcony – a rocking chair – a table – a plant pot falls – the table falls – the woman moves into frame – outside a towel floats down (it starts too high). We cut to the road, cars – feet – pan to girl's body. The tragedy around which the film revolves is established without melodrama but the effect is devastating. There is an intense parallel between this film and Bergman's *Persona* in that silence plays a large part in the drama. The past remains the subject of the film. It is about one hour into the film before the future is referred to and then it is by the old maid Anna: 'After the funeral I would like to go away for a week.'

There are many one-shot scenes, often faces are not shown at all and very seldom in close-up. Bresson's desire for stillness, silence and emptiness (whiteness) conveys the intensity of the situation. At one point he has the man and the girl at the theatre hearing Hamlet's advice to the players: 'Speak the speech I pray you.' It is Shakespeare's equivalent of Bresson's aesthetic. Later he emphasizes the point by showing the girl's disgust at how Shakespeare's text has been mangled.

43 *Une Femme Douce* embodies Robert Bresson's precept: 'Build your film on white, on silence and on stillness'

Very seldom does Bresson structure a scene by intercutting. (An exception is the soup-drinking scene when silence and stillness emphasize the emptiness between the characters.) More typical is the scene where the man is watching the girl listening to a record. We see her from over his shoulder, which is very much on the edge of frame. This shot is held for a considerable time, then the man moves his head and the newspaper he is holding very slightly, and we are reminded of his presence without a cut to the reverse angle of him watching.

GODARD *Pierrot Le Fou* (1966)
Godard, as we have already noted, is another director who has articulated the central contribution of cutting to the film process. In *Montage mon beau souci* he wrote: 'Montage is above all an integral part of mise-en-scene. Only at peril can one be separated from the other. One might as well try to separate the rhythm from the melody. . . . Editing can restore to actuality that ephemeral grace, neglected by both snob and film-lover, or can transform chance into destiny.'

For Godard, however, there has always been a degree of tension between his awareness of the power of editing and the way it functions in the conventional commercial film: 'The most that efficient editing will give a film otherwise without interest is precisely the initial impression of having been directed.' Consequently he has always been at pains to resist the seductive elements of editing technique.

Perhaps the watershed in his work was *Pierrot Le Fou*. He prefaced the film with Elie Faure's description of the work of the painter Velasquez in old age, taken from Faure's *Histoire de l'art* (1921–7), and read largely in voice-over by Ferdinand, played by Jean-Paul Belmondo:

'His only experience of the world was those mysterious copulations

which united the forms and tones with a secret but inevitable movement
. . . space reigned supreme. It was as if some tenuous radiation gliding
over the surfaces imbued itself of their visible emanations modelling
them and endowing them with forms carrying elsewhere a perfume like
an echo, which would thus be dispersed like an imponderable dusk, over
all the surrounding frames.'

At the end of the quotation we see Belmondo in his bath reading from
the book to his young daughter. Godard explained the purpose of the
quotation: 'This is the theme. Its definition . . . one should not describe
people but what lies between them.' (*Cahiers du Cinéma*, 171, 1965.) In
another scene Belmondo says to Samuel Fuller, the American film
director: 'I've always wanted to know what the cinema is.' Fuller's reply
is underlined by being translated into French by a girl. He says: 'The film
is like a battleground – love – hate – action – violence – death – in one
word "Emotion"'; to which the Belmondo character exclaims 'Ah!'. This
exchange is handled in one shot of Belmondo flanked by Fuller and the
girl, and happens at a party where all the imagery and dialogue are
concerned with the clichés of the medium of advertising. Godard
provides ample evidence of the attitude we should take to the surface
narrative. He periodically interrupts the flow to reawaken our awareness
of his lack of concern with the story as such. As Belmondo and Anna
Karina career in a car towards the Riviera, the former turns at one point
and addresses a remark to the camera. She asks whom he is talking to and
he replies: 'The audience.'

Nevertheless, Godard is not cavalier with his use of editing technique.
In this and other films, such as *Weekend* (1967), his awareness of when
the audience will expect a cut allows him to stimulate our consciousness
of the medium simply by not cutting, or shooting in such a way that the
camera movement or the movement of characters in and out of frame
substitutes for the cut. It is his confidence, when shooting, in the way
editing works, that allows him to control the way he uses the process.

ROHMER *Love in the Afternoon* (1972)
For another French director, Eric Rohmer, the space between people and
between words is even more central to his style. In the six *Contes
Moraux*, and especially in *Love in the Afternoon*, words hang in the air
between characters as if nothing that can be said is significant enough to
prevent the inevitable process of people being trapped by their own fate.
Superficially his films are empty of drama, but he allows the existence of
such a vacuum to resonate, by not cutting until we are painfully aware
that a confrontation can have no resolution. He will hold a character's
uneasy reaction to the words of another, usually in a wide shot until we
know there is nowhere to go. More often than most directors he uses the
fade out as an articulate comment on the inconclusiveness of situations.
His films are preoccupied with human relationships that remain locked
in a sterile non-communication as if socialization has guaranteed the
impossibility of his characters coming to terms with the dichotomy
between their desires and the 'rules of the game'.

In *Love in the Afternoon* the protagonist is confronted with the
nakedness of three women in his life and on each occasion he is unable to
integrate his reaction with the relationship that his social attitudes
demand. The sight of his wife in the shower is unnerving to him because

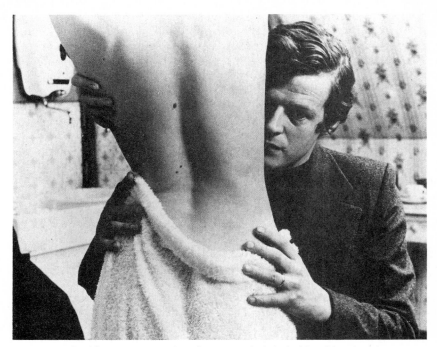

44 *Love in the Afternoon*: Eric Rohmer's protagonist is intimidated into inaction

he realizes he takes her body for granted; the au-pair rushes past him to deal with the baby and we feel his embarrassment; and the woman he wants to make love to is too much of a threat when she finally invites attention. The beauty of each scene is that Rohmer makes them seem accidental. It is as if they provoke a counter-rhythm to the mental life of the protagonist and thus become barriers to his attempts to come to terms with his own psychology. There is a richness in Rohmer's work which is almost in spite of his economic unfussy style. The camera only moves when it is unavoidable, and cutting functions as periodic punctuation rather than fracturing each moment artificially. The cut or the fade thus become important punctuation and are not used as mechanical devices.

PENN *Night Moves* (1975)

In this film the character played by Gene Hackman responds to an invitation from his wife, played by Susan Clark, to see a Rohmer movie by saying: 'No thanks, I saw a Rohmer movie once – it was like watching paint dry.' Penn, or rather Alan Sharp, the writer, would probably argue that Rohmer intimidates an audience that expects a more conventional narrative style. Rohmer and the rest of the French New Wave had articulated their awareness of the values in mainstream American cinema through the magazine *Cahiers du Cinéma*. Penn and others of his generation have, to a degree, absorbed this analysis and countered it with an intelligent reworking of the 'straight' narrative film. *Night Moves* is a case in point. Sharp believes that movies continue to feed off their own antecedents, implying that they cull from the imagery and style of other films a resonant continuum that acknowledges the tradition that has evolved – at least since the coming of sound.

Night Moves has scenes that illustrate the way a craftsman such as Penn can complement the feeling that exists in the script with a shooting style that seems to come out of the writing rather than being imposed upon it. A vital contribution to this is Dede Allen's cutting. When Hackman confronts his wife's boyfriend and asks, 'How is it between you and Ellen?', there are five cuts before the reply. They are paced so well that we are not conscious of them as cuts but only of the build-up in tension that they provide. Earlier, when Hackman sees his wife and her boyfriend come out of the cinema and go off together, his emotional response is built over twelve cuts all on medium or long shots, only coming to a close shot of Hackman as he decides finally not to confront the couple. Each shot of Hackman can be said to represent a changing emotion from pleasure at seeing his wife, through curiosity, amazement, apprehension, indicision and finally action.

The counterpoint of the progression of the couple from the front of the cinema to the boyfriend's car acts as the 'moves' provoking Hackman's changing response. What Allen has actually done is to construct a very telling parallel action sequence from what are basically only two shots. The end sequence of *Night Moves* contains a dramatic section with 22 shots in the space of 10 seconds. Detailed analysis reveals no 'cheating' in the sense that no shot, even of a few frames, is other than a relevant part of the action as the sea-plane first kills Jennifer Warren and then plunges into the sea within inches of the motor boat on which Hackman is helplessly stranded. It is a model of economic action-cutting, with none of the fussy flamboyance of earlier Penn movies, e.g. *Bonnie and Clyde* (1967), where slow motion and other devices artificially extend the moment of high drama.

These aspects of *Night Moves* indicate the availability of 'commercial' cinema for detailed dissection. Previous examples in this chapter resist such analysis. Cutting functions as a more conscious device in the conventional movie, but because this makes it more accessible we should neither be discouraged by its limitations nor use such evidence to make value judgments about style. Editing, as Eisenstein was emphasizing in the 1930s, is not about what happens at the cut but what is placed between the cuts. It is not the juxtaposition that is important but the elements that we choose to juxtapose.

POLANSKI *Chinatown* (1974)

Occasionally Hollywood and Europe meet without the tension between their stylistic traditions causing a negative result. Roman Polanski achieved a remarkable synthesis of these traditions in *Chinatown*. He had already demonstrated a sure hand in earlier films, especially in the opening sequences of *Rosemary's Baby* (1968), where the economy of exposition, while developing an atmosphere of foreboding, is founded on shooting and cutting that exhibit an admirable conviction about the right shot, its angle and size, how long it is held, and an inevitable progression from scene to scene. These values are further enhanced in the superbly scripted (by Robert Towne) and performed *Chinatown*. What Polanski has absorbed, consciously or unconsciously, can be traced back to Eisenstein's mise-en-shot principle, which allows the director to confront the way each scene works without treating the cut as the only punctuating device available to him. In a number of crucial scenes cutting

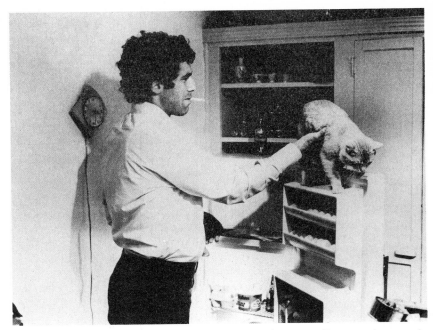

45 *The Long Goodbye:* Elliot Gould and his cat, whose prowling complements the restlessness of Robert Altman's camera

is virtually absent, but the positioning and movement of characters, and the pacing of action and dialogue, provide a rhythm that works better than editing construction could.

When Jack Nicholson, as Gittes, confronts John Huston as Noah Cross, no elaborate cover of the scene is allowed to interrupt the flow. Cuts are made only for emphasis and not as mere mechanistic devices. The same is true in Nicholson's visits to Mulwray's office – the uneasiness of the latter's secretary is conveyed by the private eye prowling in front of her in wide shot. Again when Nicholson and Faye Dunnaway are talking in bed, a static high-angle shot concentrates our attention on their exchange in a way cutting would not.

However, Polanski is not averse to cutting. The proceedings of the city council early in the film, when the new dam is being discussed, contains a number of cuts which allow us to digest information about characters and situation, while the debate is carried on in words as often as not against images of people other than the speaker. The climax of the scene, when sheep are driven into the council chamber, works well partly because the editing avoids planting such an event as the likely dénouement of the scene. *Chinatown* is the kind of film which demonstrates a real control over the kind of questions we have asked ourselves with regard to the function of editing in the total process. If the function of each scene and the focus of attention are analysed, almost no examples of loose or lazy construction are revealed. Polanski has said that he considers himself a bad writer but a good scenarist. His films, especially *Chinatown*, are cogent evidence of this.

ALTMAN *The Long Goodbye* (1972)

One American director who in recent years has consistently conducted his own exploration of the contribution of editing to his films is Robert Altman. His attitudes to camera, sound and performance as well as to editing have demonstrated his search for a more effective and interesting language. Although he is unable to make the dramatic leaps that Griffith incorporated, his work has a similar awareness of the need to expand and extend the craft. In *The Long Goodbye* he adopts radical technique. The camera is hardly, if ever, still. Sometimes the movement is marginal but it is always used to good purpose. The camera, like Elliot Gould's cat, prowls about as if restlessly seeking the only sustenance that will satisfy it. The character played by Gould deals with surface reality with as little effort as necessary, always conscious that there is something beyond the apparent that will give a clue to the mystery. Often the 'rule' that maintains that cutting on movement is difficult and dangerous is ignored, and because Altman has control over rhythm and pacing it seldom falters. The scene which culminates in the awareness of Nina von Pallandt and Gould of Sterling Hayden's drowning is handled through reflection and background action of the suicide, played against the conversation in foreground. A dog provides a restless counterpoint to the action and as it drops the dead man's walking stick we cut to the search for the body with telling conclusiveness. The tension throughout the sequence is sustained without the conventional reliance on intercutting.

Cutting and the private-eye genre

It is no accident that the last three films discussed – *Night Moves*, *Chinatown* and *The Long Goodbye* – are from the same genre. There is a natural affinity between the private-eye thriller and certain aspects of the particular contribution that editing can provide. In this genre there is invariably close identification with the detective who seems caught up in events beyond his control, and the dynamic of the film depends upon the way twists in the story are complemented by juxtapositions in the editing. The emphasis is on the visual detail and not merely on the occasional moment of high drama. Every image is potentially a clue, either to the understanding of the mystery or to feed our desire to get inside the character and motivation of the protagonist. There is a vital difference between Raymond Chandler and, say, Agatha Christie whose *Death on the Nile* (1978) remains literary and theatrical because it depends on direct verbal exposition and the melodrama of obvious and overtly threatening situations. The danger in private-eye movies is always beneath the surface of the narrative, and this allows for a uniquely cinematic structure where the cut, along with composition, camera movement and sound can carry the development of a scene while the superficial narrative is working in dialogue and action. Used in this way the cut becomes a weapon, and constructing a sequence becomes analogous to fencing where each thrust and parry gives rhythmic counterpoint to the narrative progression. The distillation of this style is the action film. In such films cutting contributes a great deal to, for instance, car chases, fights and gun battles, but in such instances the cut is usually serving the action directly rather than providing a deeper perspective.

HITCHCOCK *The Trouble with Harry* (1955)

We should be careful to avoid falling into the trap of thinking that directors working in commercial cinema are necessarily restricting themselves to being only good story-tellers. A prime example is Alfred Hitchcock, whose work it would be misguided to dismiss as simply serving the suspense film well. Although it is arguably atypical, *The Trouble with Harry* is a clear indication of the real quality of his art. A small community in New England is the setting for this black comedy which deals with the problem posed by the need to dispose of Harry's corpse – an embarrassment to all the people involved. Hitchcock is quoted in Donald Spoto's *The Art of Alfred Hitchcock* (1976) as having said: 'With Harry I took melodrama out of the pitch black night and brought it out into the sunshine. It is as if I had set up a murder by a rustling brook and spilled a drop of blood in the clear water. These contrasts establish a counterpoint, they elevate the commonplace in life to a higher level.'

Hitchcock planned every shot and the way in which each shot slotted together. The result is a predetermined matrix demonstrating a razor-sharp analysis of how to get from the page to the screen. He once said of murder: 'As you can see the best way to do it is with "scissors".' His films make that remark equally applicable to structuring the visual narrative. He did not need the corpulent silhouette or the obligatory appearance to sign his films – every cut was a confirmation of his signature. He

46 *Confrontation*: an example of the choreographed movement that is Jansco's hallmark

47 *Tokyo Story:* Yasujiro Ozu's frame transcends the convention

invariably had his scripts storyboarded (drawings for each set-up in a scene, usually defining the shot for each section of the script), and in essence this visualization represented the cutting order before the film was shot.

JANCSO *and* OZU

One further comparison will underline the contrasting approaches to editing available to directors. No starker contrast in style could be imagined than that between the Hungarian Jancso and the Japanese Yasujiro Ozu. Jancso has evolved a totally fluid style by choreographing camera and characters to substitute for the cut. Perhaps the most complete realization of his approach is *The Confrontation* (1968) in which movement becomes almost pure symbol. Ozu, on the other hand, as for example in *Tokyo Story* (1953), uses an almost exclusively static camera, framing in such a way as to demand consideration of the action outside the area shown. His characters seem almost consciously to deny the camera's presence, as when two people converse in profile facing in the same direction.

Both these directors prefer the continuous shot to the cut sequence, but neither denies the value of editing. Their response is contained in their style – with Jancso all camera movement is motivated by the action and reaction of characters, whereas Ozu provides punctuation and construction through entrances, crossing the frame and exits, often using emptiness as a rhythmic device. Despite their differences the styles of both these directors have their roots in Eisenstein's montage and mise-en-shot principles, and demonstrate dramatically why the emergent editor has to do much more than just learn to cut.

Documentary: HUMPHREY JENNINGS

During the short period when he effectively enshrined the sombre but vital feelings of Britain confronted by the Nazi threat, Jennings produced a poetic cinema which few have emulated. He wished to 'tie knots in history' by using the image as visual metaphor. His work reminds me of Emily Dickinson's axiom, 'Forever is composed of nows', for his images encapsulated a particular era as if they were being preserved in aspic.

Although his work varied from pure montage to 'constructed reality' it was in visual metaphor that he excelled. *Listen to Britain* (1941) is his most thorough realization of image as symbol. Its magical quality is related to the way he structures the imagery into a rhythm and line that seems inevitable and indeed derives its power from the inner dynamic. The way sound is used to complement the visuals without commentary (the introductory speech should not be considered as part of Jennings's conception) and without dialogue is an object lesson to all film-makers. Every image is more than a simple picture and every juxtaposition is both a natural progression and a comment. This film is constructed like a poem: its style and content are inseparable. It is propaganda, but it persuades through metaphor rather than polemic. It convinces because the images and sounds create their own resonances. It uses the cut, the mix and the fade as positive elements in the overall style. It points to the fact that film is a language that can work best when dealing with the action away from the centre of the stage, that it is one thing to portray the vortex of events but quite another to focus on the heartbeat of those who stand and wait. It is to the soul of a nation what Riefenstahl's *Triumph of the Will* (1934) was to the head. It is the affirmation that the mere capturing of reality is not a sufficient justification for film, however dramatic the events recorded may be.

Any sequence serves to illustrate the point: a quiet country village, a rumbling sound – tanks are seen disturbing the stillness – they rumble on to war – mix to sky – 'music while you work' mix to road under railway bridge with train over – industrial landscape – factory girls – tannoy radio – girls singing at work. The shot that gets the sequence moving and links from the sky to the factory is the travelling shot under the railway bridge which coincides with the train passing over. This shot was taken at Denham, down the road from where the film was being cut. Apparently Jennings and his editor, Stewart McAllister, could not decide how to get from the armoured column rumbling through the village to the factory girls and this shot was obtained during the editing. With the orchestrated sound it works like magic. The poet has found the right phrase.

Today the attitude to documentary hardly allows room for such emotionally subjective work. It claims a seriousness and responsibility that by and large eliminates the 'indulgence' of the genuine artist.

Objectivity, distance and reality

The debate about documentary in recent years has raised very important questions: the film-maker's attitude to his subjects or the people portrayed in his film, the ways in which the form can acknowledge the way the material has been obtained and, especially, how editing has manipulated that material.

The demand for accurate representation of events, and the desire to

48 Humphrey Jennings with the pianist, Dame Myra Hess, who appears in *Listen to Britain*

demonstrate in the film that manipulation has been kept to a minimum, make the cameraman's role more central and crucial. Observational documentary attempts to respect 'reality' by a rigorous application of straightforward representation. The long take, uninterrupted by cuts, not camouflaging the passage of time, not reinterpreting events through a voice-over, all lead to a shooting style that selects as the camera is turning, visibly demonstrating the point of view and the relation of the film-maker to his subject.

However, there is a danger of allowing the style itself to justify film-making. When the victims of a cruel system of punitive treatment are seen to need help in Peter Watkin's *Punishment Park* (1971), and the camera crew are merely concerned to record their suffering for the 'outside world', we are forced to consider the moral dilemma of the film-makers faced with the choice of keeping their devices trained on the subject or putting down the camera and recorder and interfering in the 'action'. The choice is seldom so polarized but it is hard to see where to draw the line. Having a camera in your hand does not make you less responsible for the people being portrayed, and the cutting room is not the place to put right the doubtful decisions made earlier. Technique is not morally neutral: no amount of aesthetic honesty can justify ethically reprehensible decisions about what is shot.

Television has encouraged the acceptance of a devalued form of documentary in which the link-man or commentator allows the form to depend on no more than journalistic juggling and a structure that is glued together with smart phrasing. The events and people portrayed are pawns to be sacrificed to a stalemate between superficial imagery and clever comment. Editing becomes debased to the level of eliminating anything that conflicts with the pat presentation and emphasizing the extremes which back up the predetermined stance, even if that stance is ostensibly neutral.

GRAEF *and* WISEMAN

The exceptions struggle to avoid fitting into the mould: the editor must fight to remain aware of what the material represents and how best to retain the spirit of it while condensing it to a length that is digestible for the audience. All editing is compromise but in documentary the important thing is to prevent editing decisions compromising the validity of the material. Roger Graef, especially in the series *Space Between Words* (1972) and *Decisions* (1976), and Fred Wiseman in such films as *High School* (1968), *Basic Training* (1971) and *Model* (1980), carry their audience by maintaining a respect for the subject of their films and by using editing as a technique that retains the feeling of the situations and attitudes of the people they portray.

In the application of technique to arrive at a satisfactory structure there are two cardinal rules. Never make a cut that calls attention to its own cleverness; in doing so you will fall prey to the arrogance and conceit that destroys your credibility as an editor. Concomitantly never divorce form from content. As Lindgren said in *The Art of the Film*: 'Form is itself a quality of content, and the more highly charged the content of a statement the more formal in character it is likely to be. To destroy the form of a line of poetry is to rob it of the most vital part of its content.'

Finally, it must be said that learning to apply the language of editing is only possible by experience of the actual process. This can be reinforced by the analysis of particular films including those of the directors I have used as examples. Their work is valuable for the specific reason that they have used editing to do more than just provide an efficient narrative structure. I would encourage those readers who are able to, to spend as much time as possible in careful and detailed analysis of individual films.

6   Sound in editing

The use of sound in editing is referred to in many contexts in this book. However, I make no apology for devoting a specific chapter to it. Although film still depends largely on sound for its dramatic effectiveness, the 'art' of sound is largely neglected and its function underestimated. Ironically, most films are a slave to sound, yet during the making of those films it is considered of secondary importance.

One of my most vivid memories of a response to a film I had cut was by Edith Vogel, the famous pianist and music teacher. After the viewing she commented: 'Very nice, but not enough silences.' It was a very important point. The most frequent questions asked when laying the sound tracks for a film are: how shall we fill this bit? or, what can we put here? Filling the silence is the worst approach imaginable to the creation of a sound track. Just as everything that appears in the visual frame should be meant, so everything that is heard should also be meant. Cluttered sound tracks are a definite indication that the film-makers have not understood how sound can best be used to support the images.

We do well also to remember that *all* sound has its own rhythms and cadences which often prove intractable in relation both to images and other sounds. This is fairly obvious with regard to music but less apparent with the spoken word and effects. Rain on a window pane can sound everything from sad to threatening. Words, especially in English, often depend for their actual meaning on emphasis, inflections and tone. But as well as having certain innate qualities that we must learn to respect, sound also has a degree of flexibility unavailable to us in the fixed images that are our raw material for editing. A director such as Altman has learned to layer his sound in a masterly fashion using changing perspective, sound beyond the visual frame and interwoven, overlapping tracks. It is to this sophisticated level we must aspire, and there is no doubt that the cutting room has a major part to play.

One factor that is easily neglected is the effect of your cutting-room equipment on sound, both in the perception of its quality and in the maintenance of that quality. If you are lucky enough to work with high-quality equipment, including amplification and speakers, then there is less likelihood of rude shocks awaiting you in the dubbing theatre. However, the function of sound heads on editing machinery is limited: their narrow and 'toppy' response can give totally misleading reproduction. This is one good reason why projecting your film, from sync rushes onward, are of as much value for sound as they are for picture.

These sound heads are a source of other potential trouble too. If they are worn or misaligned or if contact between the head and the track is too hard during traverse the actual oxide will wear thin and the signal will inevitably deteriorate. If too little attention is paid to this, tracks may reach the dubbing theatre in a deplorable state. In feature films there is no reason for such things to occur, since the sound editor is continually monitoring the quality of all sound that is likely to be used for the final film, and fresh transfers will be ordered from the original $\frac{1}{4}$-in. tapes for any sub-standard sections.

It is important to establish the way your sound track should function during cutting. Editors' attitudes to sound vary enormously. There are those who will even cut dialogue scenes *mute* having once digested the words and their rhythm. There are those who follow the words as the pegs to hang the structure on. There are also those who orchestrate their sound track from the word go, never having only *one* track with which to view the cutting copy.

Whatever facility you have to cut on – be it a Steenbeck 6 plate with two tracks or even a Compeditor with four tracks – the most vital thing is that you decide in cutting what particular sound is most important at any particular moment in the film. Of course there are times when, for instance, the layering of sound is imperative to a sequence before you can judge its effectiveness, or when voice-over or music have to be laid alongside the sync track. But often there is a temptation to lay a second track in the belief that it will transform something that is not working into a totally convincing scene. What actually happens is that the second sound element adds a certain concreteness, and thus appears to prove the validity of the scene. This is especially true of music, and is a very seductive and dangerous way of obscuring the real problems in cutting. Indeed, even scenes which are intended to be covered by music alone should *always* be cut mute first: they will be all the stronger if the visuals have had to stand on their own before music is added. Obviously this does not apply where the music is sync or playback.

Working with one track in this way makes the most of flexibility in cutting. There is a psychological inhibition, partly stemming from the physical effort required, about radically altering more than one element of sound. Working with more than one track also makes projection of the film very difficult as I believe the cut should be viewed several times as it is being refined.

It is also true that to leave a shot or shots mute in the cutting of a sequence *can* be dangerous. Judging the overall flow of a scene is made impossible by sudden loss of sound. It may have been felt unnecessary to shoot a reaction shot in sync but when the scene is cut you should try to use part of the sync track over the mute shot or insert a suitable wild track, or else the rhythm will be interrupted. If you leave this until tracklaying you may get a rude shock at a time when making picture alterations is not the priority.

CATEGORIES OF SOUND

There are four main types of sound: dialogue, effects, narration or voice-over and music. The chart on p. 97 gives an indication of the origins from which these sounds can be acquired (the more normal sources are asterisked):

	DIALOGUE	EFFECTS	VOICE-OVER	MUSIC
Sync	/★	/★	/	/★
Wild track	/	/★	/★	/
Post-sync	/★	/★	–	–
Playback	–	–	–	/★
Library	–	/★	/	/
Special recording	–	/	/★	/★

Perhaps the most interesting aspect of such a chart is that potentially all kinds of sound can be obtained from several sources. The way a final sound track is created for a film can vary enormously. In major feature film the profile is normally as follows:

DIALOGUE:	*Sync* and/or *Post-sync*
EFFECTS:	*Wild track* and/or *Post-sync*
VOICE-OVER:	*Special recording*
MUSIC:	*Playback* and/or *Special recording*

However, in a documentary that is attempting to convey the impression that the total film is built out of elements innate to the subject being filmed, *all* sound may be sync with perhaps occasional wild tracks recorded during the shooting.

Elsewhere I have expressed my own preference for sync recording as the bedrock of a good sound track and also described the value of good wild tracks (see p. 37). Early awareness of the quality or usability of all recordings made during shooting is essential since efforts will have to be made to replace unsatisfactory essential sound. In this chapter I will concentrate on the sources of sound other than those used during shooting.

DIALOGUE

Of the three sources of dialogue listed above I regard sync as by far the most preferable, wild but matched recording during the period of shooting as second-best and post-sync as a poor substitute. Synchronous recording of dialogue has already been dealt with in detail. Here I will outline the procedure for post-synchronization.

At the outset it must be determined what sections of the film require post-synchronization. This is best done as soon after shooting as possible to maximize the chances of the artists' availability, unless the suggestion is to revoice (i.e. to replace the artist's voice with that of another), which can be done at any time. (Remember, however, that such replacement may cause offence to the original artist, indeed could even lead to writs being served!)

It is not feasible – least of all on exteriors – to post-sync the odd line or two from a scene or even one character and not the others, as a very noticeable change in ambience or background atmosphere usually results. So the decision has to be totally to accept or reject the voice tracks for each scene. But it is often possible to replace fluffs, unclear words or even unsatisfactory readings of whole phrases by using the sound from another take, carefully laid to match the sync as closely as possible.

Once the scenes to be post-synchronized have been determined and a booking made in a recording theatre, you must then carefully analyse the scenes so that they can be broken down into convenient segments. The usual method of post-sync is by 'looping': the relevant section of the picture and guide track where available are removed from the cutting copy and joined head to tail in short sections with a short leader in between. Each section is matched with a length of virgin sound stock. The creation of these loops allows constant and immediate replaying of the sections for rehearsal and recording until director and editor are satisfied that the performance is acceptable and the words in close enough synchronization to be convincing (allowing for some adjustment that is usually possible back in the cutting room). The best system I have encountered is using 35 mm loops for the virgin stock, whether the picture is 35 mm or 16 mm. If the recording studio has a 35 mm triple-track facility you are given real flexibility, since during recording you will be able to switch tracks instantaneously, holding at least two versions while recording in the third position. This gives choice when laying up and the chance to cut between different takes if preferred. Furthermore, on 35 mm you have four times the precision of adjustment available as there are four perforations to each frame compared with only one on 16 mm magnetic stock. 16 mm sound stock is now available with two perforations to the frame, thus giving double flexibility when laying up.

The editor has to make crucial decisions about where to divide the scene when 'looping'. Ideally the natural rhythm of the scene should be respected and not interrupted unnecessarily but, for both mechanical and practical reasons, there is a limit to the length the loop can be. Somewhere between 20 and 30 seconds is best: much less allows for no development of performance, much more can be exhausting if it is going to take numerous rehearsals and takes to get an acceptable replacement track.

Every word of dialogue must now be transcribed and broken down into separate 'cues'. 'Cues' are signified on the picture by a diagonal line drawn across the frames over a length of about one second, finishing just before the first modulation on the guide track of the phrase being cued. One sound editor I know recommends stopping the line four frames before the first modulation to allow for the fact that the artist may find it hard to hit the cue and thus tend to hurry the first word or two to catch up. If there is more than one artist, the cue lines can be drawn running alternate ways across the film for differentiation. A new cue should be given each time there is a gap in the dialogue, not just where there is a new sentence.

If there is a guide track this can be listened to by the artist through ear-phones, at least during rehearsal; for the take itself the guide track may interfere with any attempt to 'improve' or 'change' the interpretation. (Beyond a certain point such 'improvements' can be dangerous as the mood and feel of the picture will only allow a certain amount of variation in the speech patterns.)

The decision to post-synchronize artists together or separately is a delicate one. It is important to know how experienced each is at this technique, but you will be surprised at how quickly a novice will pick it up, especially if working with someone who has done it before. If the artists have a rapport from having performed the scene when it was filmed it is usually best to trade on that familiarity. You will find that post-synchronization highlights the existence of two very different kind of actors: the 'classical' who decides on an interpretation of each role and proceeds to refine it marginally each time it is performed, and the 'intuitive' who is forever searching for new and more vivid meanings in the words and actions of a character. The latter can be a fairly awkward customer at a post-sync session!

Anyone expecting the revelation of hidden qualities and meaning through post-synchronization will almost certainly be disappointed. It can only produce an improvement where the quality of the original is unusable. It is also an added expense unless it was decided on in advance and shooting time was saved because a good recording was not needed. If, when shooting, you know that post-synchronization will be necessary, remember to record atmosphere tracks to use as backing – they make studio dialogue that much more credible, especially when the scene is exterior.

EFFECTS

Looping for the post-synchronization of effects has other requirements. Cueing should still be done where appropriate, but the first things to remember are facilities and props. Footsteps are commonly involved and the studio must possess a variety of surfaces to match those in the film. Ideally concrete, asphalt, gravel, sand and wood should be available and troughed so that each can be dampened to simulate wet conditions. Each trough should be a couple of yards long to avoid the impression of 'running on the spot'. Footwear should be similar to that used in the film. If you engage specialists they will bring with them a whole range of footwear and other useful items. Most theatres possess a miniature door for replacement purposes on exits and entrances. More awkward doors and gates must be contrived or recorded elsewhere. The noise of cutlery, crockery and chairs are commonly required and these must be supplied as necessary.

Whereas I tend to be dismissive about the value of post-sync dialogue, if detail can be matched in the visuals, post-sync effects can bring considerable bonuses that could not have come across in a sync recording where the balance of one microphone was geared to a good dialogue track. An interior that has been well-shot on a set can convince an audience of being a real room until someone opens or shuts a door. Heightened perspective on eating and drinking or the shutting of a door, even if out of frame, can contribute considerable ambience to a scene.

To sum up the important points about post-synchronization of dialogue and effects for the editor:

1   An early decision to go for post-sync is invaluable to secure artists.
2   Sequences to be looped must be broken down and cued in convenient lengths.
3   Transcripts must be provided for artists, recordists, editor and director.
4   A record should be kept of the best takes if a choice is available.
5   All loops should be marked according to a simple numbering system, e.g. 1P1, where 1 stands for reel 1, P for picture and 1 for the first

loop in that reel. 1G/T1 would thus be the guide track for that loop and 1V1 the virgin for the same.

6   It is important to fold loops carefully to avoid kinking. They should not be wound too tightly and should be rolled up so that the join is left on the outside. These should be clipped or taped to avoid unravelling and stored, preferably with all the material for each loop (i.e. picture, guide track and virgins) in separate cans.

7   It is best to make the virgins totally of sound stock with no spacer or leader in between. This allows for useful studio atmosphere to be recorded front and end of the picture section, thus preventing gaps when the recorded track is adjusted for sync in the cutting room.

8   Remember also to list 'props' required when recording effects.

VOICE-OVER OR NARRATION

If this has to be specially recorded, it is best done to picture to ensure that length, positioning and effect are going to work. If possible, the effectiveness of narration should be tested by recording a guide track in advance of bringing in the narrator. It is in any case essential to test each section carefully against the picture. When recording to picture you should annotate the typescript with front and end footages to ensure correct timing. Without picture, timings should be supplied and a stop-watch used to check the lengths while recording. Words may have to be dropped or added if a reasonable change of pace fails to give a good fit on any particular section.

Choosing the right voice is not easy. If there are other voice-overs then there must be sufficient contrast to avoid confusion and to differentiate between the 'objective' narration and 'subjective' voices. It is easy to assume that an authoritative voice will lend that quality to an otherwise unconvincing film. In fact, such a voice may actually emphasize the less than convincing visuals. The best guide is to determine in your own mind the tone and mood of the piece. Deciding between male and female should be a matter of common sense, although subtle alterations in effect can be achieved by changing the sex of the speaker even though the words remain the same.

The most important decision, however, is whether to use narration at all and, if so, what purpose it serves. In these days when dramatic and documentary film are always borrowing elements from each other's styles, narration/voice-over/commentary are being used in a much more interesting way. The first-person voice-over adopted by a number of feature films as a natural extension of the Raymond Chandler or Dashiell Hammett private-eye, commenting on situations they are trying to deal with/get out of/run away from, is the traditional approach. All you need is Elliot Gould or, in a previous generation, Humphrey Bogart, seeming to be unable to control events that they accidentally or casually get involved in and the narration becomes a natural element. This allows the director to keep his audience in touch with things which are difficult (or expensive) to show, at the same time as conveying a feeling of identification with the thoughts of the protagonist. It also enables insights to be revealed that the visuals do not convey, thus layering the superficial with 'meaning', especially if the words are spare and ambivalent.

Narration used in this way will always function best if preconceived, so that the shooting incorporates and allows for its eventual addition. You can give your film a very particular flavour by deciding which character is going to tell the story on the sound track. The girl's narration in Robert Mulligan's *To Kill a Mockingbird* (1963) and, more recently, Terence Malick's *Badlands* (1973), lend a deceptively innocent air to the way we view the events portrayed. Remember though that if you choose such a 'direct' method of letting the audience in on the story you will inevitably shut off certain options, and relying on voice-over to carry the plot may give the impression of cheating and avoiding visual exposition. However, like any good device, if it is integrated well into the fabric of your film, first-person voice-over can be a valuable asset.

The third-person narrator has now lost favour amongst film-makers. It is recognized as a literary device that does not transfer easily, least of all to dramatic film. It has a certain quaintness unless associated with events rather than emotions. War films can always be introduced with a voice-over statement of dates, places and deployment of forces, although a caption would do just as well. Documentary, especially in television, is still dominated by the 'Voice of God' technique. The words, nay usually the Presence of the revered Pundit, are what makes the conventional documentary supposedly credible and also, incidentally, is usually the only cement holding together the disparate elements that make up the visuals. There is obviously much more to documentary use of narration or voice-over than this. Especially valuable is the use of wild-track description of events, or the background to them, by a participant or someone we know, from evidence in the film, to be privy to knowledge that is useful in understanding or appreciating the events portrayed.

Except for films that are strictly concerned with detailing a process and thus require an exact description in words and pictures of what goes on, voice-over should always be seen as an opportunity to say what cannot be shown, or to counterpoint the images with words that cast a new light on the pictures. Still, it is no coincidence that the traditional voice-over is the most frequently imitated or parodied element in film technique, producing some of the funniest cartoons, television sketches and feature sequences just by playing a commentary dead-pan. For, without discretion and conviction, even the most serious use of narration will become unintentionally funny and destroy rather than support your thesis or structure.

The worst kind of narration is where the pictures are shot subsequent to the 'expert' writing the voice track. This almost inevitably becomes the equivalent of a slide-show which has little or nothing to do with film-making. The best voice-over is spare, economic, allusory rather than direct, cathartic in its effect on the images, and questioning rather than answering. In this way it becomes a stimulus rather than a solution, and points rather than leads the audience.

It is worth comparing narration with captions doing the same job:

	VOICE-OVER	CAPTION
1	Gives tone and colour and emphasis to the words.	Allows neutral 'reading' but is cold and depersonalized.
2	Prevents the 'flow' of other voice tracks.	Requires superimposition or interruption of pictures.

3 Can be read at speed and in manner determined by director.	Must be kept on screen long enough for 'average' reader.
4 Allows positioning on shots to precise words.	Only relates directly to shots before and after.
5 Easy to record and place for fine cutting.	Needs shooting and/or optical dupe before effect can be judged.
6 Useful as links into and out of sync or wild statements which are not coherent in themselves.	If kept to factual background can add to credibility of film and its maker's attitude.

MUSIC

The use of music in film is often unsatisfactory. It is an easy – but dangerous – assumption that there are basic aspects of film and music which allow for a confluence of purpose and style so that the one may mesh with the other. Bresson has very strong views about the effect of music on film: 'It isolates your film from the life of your film (musical delectation). It is a powerful modifier and even destroyer of the real, like alcohol or dope.' He has also said: 'People flood a film with music. They are preventing us from seeing that there is nothing in those images.' His decision was to have 'no music as accompaniment, support or reinforcement'. (*Notes on Cinematography*, 1977.)

Music isolates your film from the life of your film. This isolation or separation can be emotional, stylistical, rhythmical or it can relate to pace. Music establishes its own existence just as soon as it takes shape between the composer's brain, his hand holding the pen and the manuscript paper. Music is a formal abstraction and as such has an inherent coherence which is stronger and more immediate (though not necessarily more superficial) than the other elements which make up narrative film. Unless you are able to give your visual construction and its attendant sound elements, especially dialogue and synchronous effects, the same metaphorical strength, music will dominate, indeed eclipse, the film. Since reducing your narrative to abstraction is self-defeating, the only real answer is for the music to remain unmusical in the sense of eschewing melody and the other elements of composition which make it discrete and self-sufficient. The ideal music for film has to be that which makes no sense played separately from the film of which it is supposed to be part.

In George Roy Hill's *Butch Cassidy and the Sundance Kid* (1969), the morning after Butch and the Kid have spent a night at Etta's place, Butch rides around the yard on a bike. This becomes a sequence cut to 'Raindrops are Falling on My Head'. Although this represents a happy interlude in the uneasy life of the outlaws, the song interrupts totally the flow of the film and effectively prevents the pursuance of a narrative line beyond the particular sequence. A more recent example was the song 'Bright Eyes' in *Watership Down* (1978) which did exactly the same disservice to the aesthetic of the film – the animators even changed the style of the cartoon just for that sequence. Commercially both songs probably helped the films but aesthetically they were mistakes.

The way music fails in film terms is much harder to demonstrate when we are talking of other than best-selling popular songs. Sometimes an existing piece of classical music is used as theme and background for

49 The epic imagery of Sergei Eisenstein's *Alexander Nevsky* for which Prokofiev provided a score which is superbly integrated into the film

a feature film in the belief that a priori Mozart, Brahms or Richard Strauss are bound to improve the films they are applied to. The music used in Bo Widenberg's *Elvira Madigan* (1967) and Stanley Kubrick's *2001 – A Space Odyssey* (1968) are well-known examples of this practice. A shot of the Eiffel Tower and a few bars of accordion music are still used to signify Paris although a television comedy series had the cheek to use a picture of Blackpool Tower instead. There is constant exploitation of the eminently available classical repertoire as easy pickings for the film-maker.

The reasons for this wrong-headed tendency are not too difficult to discern: laziness, ignorance, anxiety and, of course, poverty. The lazy director and editor think music of an accepted quality is an easy answer to covering any sequence which does not hang together on its own merits. The ignorant director and editor are not aware of either the deleterious effect of such music or the alternatives. The anxious director and editor need to support their material in a prestigious and snobbish way. The poor director and editor prefer to find a disc on which there are no royalties to pay, rather than to explore the possibilities of music composed and or played especially for the film, or to make the film work without music.

You may be thinking by now that I am implacably against music in film. This is far from the truth – but only if music is used carefully. If music can be counterpoint to action; if it can support without taking over; if it can substitute for other sound (e.g. effects); if it can heighten where tension already exists, or quieten when silence has won; if it can

50 Morricone's music complemented the spare imagery of Leone's *Fistful of Dollars*

emphasize its own absence by its presence – then music is to be encouraged. The composition of such music for films is a discrete art form, and should be encouraged by music schools everywhere. Only by such encouragement to understand the particular needs of film will we begin to break down this parasitical and irrelevant reliance on both the classics and derivations from the popular form. If Prokofiev can do it for Eisenstein, Britten for Grierson and, in the commercial idiom, Morricone for Leone, then it should be possible throughout film-making. After all Prokofiev as Eisenstein acknowledged, had the ability to use music as a substitute for all other forms of sound. Are we still content to plagiarize and pirate our music for film?

Let us assume that you have decided to make use of specially composed music for at least part of your film. The first thing to realize is that you do not need a full symphony orchestra for effective accompaniment to your visuals and other sound. Indeed, a piano and percussion occasionally augmented by another particular instrument can be far more effective than an over-elaborate score which swamps the film. You should also not look for a melodic line that becomes a theme: any progression of notes which is catchy enough to hum after one or two hearings is again a distraction from the film itself.

Epic music for 'epic' films is usually expected to work with a formula usually containing three themes: one for the hero, one for the romantic couple and one for the 'cause' or the larger dramatic conflict. The contrast between this and, for instance, scores for Bergman's films is considerable. His scores have the integration lacking in epic films. He is a man much concerned with silence, indeed he is also on record as admiring Bresson. There are wonderful and terrible silences in his films, and it is sometimes possible to say that these are created by music.

At what point should it be decided whether to use music? Unless the music relates to the scene in some direct way, I would suggest that the decision should usually be taken at the fine cut. Not, that is, when everything is set in concrete, but at a point when the visual material has been made to work on its own, although of course with the support of dialogue and other sync sound. Never be reduced to thinking that a scene will be all right when the music is on it because it will not be if it is not 'all right' without the music.

Perhaps the best thing music does is to support or emphasize the mood or atmosphere of a scene, but the composer must pick up resonances in the film itself and carry them on, rather than let the music act as the clue for the audience. Georges Delerue does this very well in films such as Truffaut's *Jules et Jim* (1961), where there is a real partnership, which seems almost conscious, between the characters in the film and the music as if the music represents the director. That is, *not* what the director wants the audience to think about a scene, but what he, the director, thinks about it – a much more interesting point of view!

The challenge of making music an integral part of a film has led to some interesting solutions. Lindsay Anderson's *O Lucky Man!* (1972) starts with Alan Price being seen as a sort of chorus or troubadour commenting, in vision and as music-over, on the situations that the hero, Malcom McDowell, finds himself in. Eventually McDowell meets up with Price and his group of musicians, gets a lift back to London and becomes friendly with Helen Mirren who is a sort of group mascot. In

51 In *Jules et Jim* Georges Delerue succeeded in using music to support the atmosphere without taking over the drama

this way the use of the music is up-front, overt, direct. Price's lyrics and driving style are an objectivization of McDowell's personal experience. So the score is informative and also available to Anderson as a pacing device. It is not by accident that Anderson is seen at one point in the recording studio during a number.

Feelings which are impossible to express in words often get transmuted into musical communication, especially through one or other performer sitting down at the piano! People go to concerts, listen to records, hum tunes, whistle, all in the service of using music as an expressive device. Never ignore the value of a musical element being part of the scene rather than just a superimposed score.

If music is to be specially composed and recorded, careful preparations must be made. The composer should first be shown the whole film and given an indication of where music is desired. If he is any good he will have suggestions of his own about mood and instrumentation. Exact timings will be supplied in minutes and seconds (footages are no good to someone working away from footage counters) with the music 'cues' numbered and described. The procedure from here to the final recording of the music can vary quite considerably. It is fairly certain that, given the time and opportunity, at least one more session will be held when the composer will go over his suggestions with the aid of a piano, preferably in a sound studio where the picture can be run.

Perhaps the most important thing to watch and listen for is duplication of emphasis and effect. If a cut, a word, an action or reaction are achieving the dramatic effect required, do not allow music to be wasted doing the same job. This is not so simple as it sounds since such confluence of effect seems superficially correct. If you remind yourself that the film is not meant to be a melodrama, there is a good chance you will draw back from unnecessary and unhelpful musical excesses. You should be looking to music to supply the emotion or tension directly or by counterpoint that is not present in the pictures or other sound, rather than to underline that which is being shown or described by other means. In *Montage mon beau souci* Godard refers to music as 'sounds which have the value of images – I have never used music otherwise. It plays the same role as black in Impressionist painting.'

Eventually a score is arrived at and the cutting room must prepare the sections for projection. If possible music 'cues' should be looped as for post-synchronization. Cue lines should be given for each start and for important moments in the section. Some studios and composers like to use what are called click tracks. These are a mechanical and precise substitute for a metronome, providing a constant beat to allow the composer/conductor to pace the recording.

Do not assume that music thus obtained will necessarily be appropriate. It is often very hard for a composer to judge the director's intentions, but he must settle for some interpretation in order to translate the drama into musical terms. So at a recording it is imperative that the director and editor are quick to point out if music is tending to change the emphasis in a way that is undesirable.

Perhaps the hardest thing is to know where to start and finish a piece of music to achieve the required effect. In film we can choose whether to signal events, feelings, reaction, changes, either by visual or aural means or by both. If we use both, they can be simultaneous or – better still – one can precede the other. Not only this but by cutting *and* by using different kinds and levels of sounds we can create a complex series of relationships between the events and emotions being portrayed.

In documentary film you may sometimes acquire music as background to actuality. The temptation here is to use it as a prop to your narrative line, to include it as background before and after the scene it strictly applies to, or to make a virtue of intercutting with differing perspectives on the music track. Such techniques can be successful, but your starting point should be the attitude that considers music discrete to its own context. In fact, one of the most pleasing aspects of good use of music stems from the simple technique of laying it to start 'late' and finish 'early', thus allowing a scene to establish itself *without* music and to conclude in the quiet after a period of harmonious support. Delerue is very good at this, but then he is a 'movie maniac' anyway, so saturated in film that it seems right to him to let the scene be seen to be inspiring the music rather than being slave to it.

One further point on music: there is no virtue in cutting on the beat. Nor is there any principle worth expounding about how to avoid doing so. However, it is a similar problem to cutting on visual action. The answer to both can be ascertained by first deciding what you are cutting for, i.e. what 'action' or what 'phrase' you want to emphasize or avoid emphasizing by cutting. Then imagine what time is required to be conscious of the action or phrase. This is entirely subjective but has the useful effect of avoiding the impression that the music is pulling the visuals along which will certainly appear to be the case if you cut on or, even worse, after the beat.

An editor I once knew had a simple solution to the problem of the beat. He started out by making his cuts on a music montage exactly to the beat. Then to help himself decide how many frames he should advance the picture, he invented a mental sliding scale with Bach at one end and Debussy at the other. He came into my cutting room one day looking very worried – someone had asked him to use Tchaikovsky's orchestral suite *Mozartiana* and he could not place it on his scale!

PLAYBACK

When music is being used in performance, either sung, played or for dance sequences, it is usual to pre-record the score and playback the track during shooting. On feature films and for special musical television films, the cutting room is usually required to prepare the tracks for these playback sessions. The music is recorded under optimum conditions on to a master ¼-in. tape with a sync reference. A copy is made in sync with the addition of countdown leaders for each section that is being shot. This involves the director and the choreographer or music director deciding in advance how the sequences are to be broken down into individual shots. So copies must be made from the music master for each section, always allowing slightly more music than is required. Although the technique can vary slightly the basic requirement is for a countdown and clap followed by a pause and a further countdown to the music start. So the tape might have at the beginning 3 – 2 – 1 CLAP – 3 – 2 – 1, then the music. It is also valuable to add 3 – 2 – 1 CLAP at the end for further sync reference. The countdown should be in the same rhythm as the music.

In shooting, the copy playback track is started with the camera locked in sync, the clapper is inserted in sync in vision and the whole is re-recorded as a guide track. Before cutting commences a transfer from the guide track and the master film copy are rubber-numbered in sync to enable precise laying up when the cutting is finished. In addition to the countdown, it is invaluable to identify each section in order, and even to announce the bars of music that the section covers. This numbering will coincide with a copy of the score that has been marked up bar by bar.

The advantages of playback are that it guarantees a high-quality, 'clean' recording and allows other sounds such as dialogue and effects to be obtained separately without being tied to exact and predetermined places in the score. It is possible to shoot dance sequences to a click track or metronome equivalent, but the artists then suffer from having to perform to a clinical rhythm rather than to the track which evokes the real atmosphere of the scene.

It is interesting that silent films were often shot with musicians playing appropriate music during the shooting to help the artists appreciate the mood. Even today it is not unknown for a director to use music on the set for sequences that demand a highly charged atmosphere. I well remember Stravinsky's *The Rite of Spring* being played back during the shooting of a particularly frenetic scene in Ken Russell's *The Devils* (1971). When the visuals had been shot the sound editor was allowed access to the performers for the recording of appropriate wild tracks. The actual music was, of course, composed and recorded later.

TRACKLAYING

Sound of all varieties is gathered together for one final objective: the mix. To this end, when the 'cut' has been approved the next job for the editor is tracklaying. This needs to be done meticulously. Failure to pay attention to detail and precision when tracklaying can cause chaos and disaster at the mixing session. Remember that you are dealing with the synchronous and asynchronous sounds that are meant finally to complement in all their richness the visuals of your film. It is possible to end up with upwards of a score of separate tracks, each with important sound elements to be meshed into the balanced whole. In a matter of a few hours, using the combined aural response of director, editor and mixer and the hands of the latter, one strip of magnetic track must be used to contain the right relative values of those myriad sounds. From this it can be seen that the objective of tracklaying is to provide the sounds in a form which maximizes the chance of getting the best mix. The ideal situation is to avoid the necessity of expecting the dubbing theatre, in advance, to come up with the answer to sound-track problems.

For some, tracklaying is a chore, and it is true that on occasions its satisfactions are too subtle to be discernible. But not least of them is the pleasure of providing the raw material for a smooth and efficient mixing session. Given access to good-quality sound a few simple procedural points will virtually guarantee good use of the dubbing theatre.

You must always be aware of the physical condition of your tracks. There are three aspects to watch: the joins, the perforations and wear of the oxide itself. Ideally all tracks should be pristine copies from master material. Since this entails considerable expense on stock and transfers, it is unlikely that you will experience such luxury except as a sound editor on feature films. This means that care of your tracks throughout the process of cutting is essential. To ensure that your tracks are in good condition when you reach the dubbing theatre it is important to observe the following points:

1 When synchronizing and viewing rushes check that the transfers are at the correct sound level. Low 'level' tracks will inevitably lead to trouble with background noise in the mix.
2 Ensure that all joins and rejoins are well made with no excess tape and with no gap or overlap at the join.
3 Use only one joiner otherwise you will probably find that recutting results in the creation of a gap or overlap, because of variations in the alignment of the guillotine.
4 Do not clean the joiner with metal objects since it will easily become magnetized, resulting in 'clicks' or 'bumps' at the joins.
5 Avoid running on machines or projectors where the tension is too great as this will stretch the joins and eventually cause re-perforation of the stock.
6 Keep your sound heads clean and avoid getting chinagraph or other dirt on the track, otherwise the track will become worn and damaged causing deterioration of the signal and 'drop outs'.
7 It is advisable to cut your sound diagonally to ensure a smoother transition at the join.

If, having observed the above, you reach the point of tracklaying and need to replace pieces of track for some reason, take care to match them carefully, especially for sync, and always transfer slightly more than you need to allow overlaps.

Dialogue
Having set up the cutting copy and track on your synchronizer with at least one roll of spacing, the first job is to mark up your leaders with proper sync marks and to allow several feet on the head for lace up. Clearly identify the existing track and your roll of spacing as DIALOGUE 1 and 2. The function of this first operation is to split the dialogue into two tracks and to note at the same time all requirements for wild tracks and, if necessary, further dialogue tracks. You may have narration and post-sync dialogue already inserted, both of which should go on separate tracks. Whatever you do it is as well to deal with one aspect at a time, so if you are merely splitting dialogue your original track will still contain other sound elements to be split off later.

Splitting has the prime functions of allowing the mixer to balance the dialogue and also to permit creative use of the overlap. (Some editors prefer to split their dialogue last, using the cutting track as a guide for laying all other sound.) If your trims are properly filed, each junction of dialogue is an opportunity to provide a smooth transition. With coded sync material it is a simple task to find the next section of sound, both head and tail and, as you split, to add a few frames at either end, taking care to retain the original sync at the cut. Normally the addition will contain only the background atmosphere, giving the mixer the chance to match levels and equalize if necessary. However, there are some cases where the overlap can contribute considerably more to the final track. If

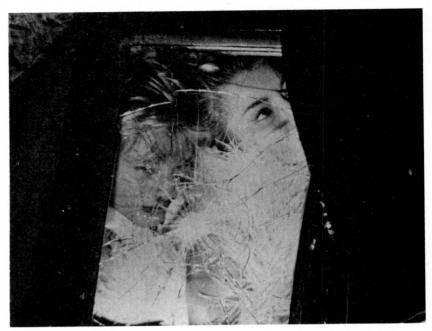

52 The climax to the opening of Joseph Losey's *Accident*, after a slow and deliberate build-up of sound effects off-screen

you have cut dialogue very tight even the breath on the front can be useful. Sometimes footsteps or other effects are only audible on one of the two shots being intercut, and the overlap allows their insertion. Occasionally some lines are 'off-mike' in the section used and these can be replaced by 'on-mike' lines from another slate, even if this means splitting *within* a shot. If the dialogue is 'loose', removal of heavy background between phrases and replacement with specially recorded atmosphere or buzz track can heighten the feeling of a scene. There is a practice in feature films called 'stripping' where all sounds other than dialogue are removed and replaced by wild tracks obtained either at the time of shooting, by post-sync or recorded by the sound editor. Never assume that because you are dealing with intercut shots all recorded in the same situation, they do not require splitting. Mike positioning, closeness of shot, relation to background, level of recording, variation in voice intensity, all contribute differences that the mixer must deal with. Indeed, never make your splitting coterminous with picture cuts. Sometimes a conversation between two people has to be split even if covered in a two-shot, to allow the opportunity to balance the voices and their background levels. So the best attitude is never to assume that what seems like a smooth sound transition on the editing machine will also appear so in the dubbing theatre. For this reason a running of the film in the mixing studio prior to tracklaying can be of great value.

Effects
If for any reason there are specific effects that have not been recorded during the shooting, these can be obtained from sound libraries and

53 Donald Sutherland holds his drowned daughter at the climax of the opening scene of *Don't Look Now*, after a gripping build-up of tension achieved with carefully controlled and disturbing imagery and sound that excludes dialogue

dubbing theatres. However, it is very dangerous to rely on these sources for adequate substitutes.

Effects should be dealt with in two distinct categories: atmospheres and specific or 'spot' effects ('spot' referring to the need for accurate placement when laying up). Atmospheres can be further divided into general and particular. Often the mistake is made of treating all atmospheres as general, and making loops to be run as background to the whole of a sequence. This can be a wasted opportunity and even a problem if the 'specifics' are not considered. Even country atmosphere or distant town traffic can contain variations that should be taken advantage of. Remember that any distinct sound in a loop will recur at regular intervals and seem artifical, even comical.

The best approach is to go through the film noting all effects required: not just the ones that are needed to match what is seen, but any pertinent sounds that might enliven the background track. You can overdo this: all effects must be used with discretion as some sounds are inevitably clichés. The cuckoo over springtime countryside is an obvious example. On the other hand, the dramatic opening of Losey's *Accident* (1967) depends upon sound effects culminating in a car crash off-screen. By careful orchestration and concentration on a 'neutral' visual of a house seen from the front gates we are impelled to listen for sound clues and subjected to an intense build-up of tension which is somehow 'relieved' by the crash. Furthermore the gap or silence before anyone emerges from the house as a response to the crash is effective because it makes the audience feel impotent in face of the inaction. An interesting comparison both visually and aurally can be made between this opening sequence and that of *Don't Look Now* (1973) by Nicolas Roeg. In this film parallel action between the parents working indoors and their little girl playing in the garden culminates in the father failing to save his daughter from drowning. The imagery is carefully controlled and sound is used as a very effective support to the tragedy, without dialogue being resorted to. Both are masterly expositions of the event around which the film narrative is built. Neither opening scene as it turns out is the 'subject' of the film – indeed one is in fact a sort of resolution and the other 'merely' a starting point.

It is worth being extremely fussy with effects. Some people even categorize their sound into homogeneous varieties and use a *separate* track for each type. At the very least, it is important that you present the mixer with effects that are not a rag-bag intercut without sufficient gaps on the same track. Gun shots, bird calls, footsteps, doors slamming and bells ringing, to give a few examples, all have to be handled differently and therefore need enough space for proper handling.

When cutting in specific effects, be careful to remove all extraneous, unwanted sound from before and after the effect itself. On the other hand, do not remove echo or reverberation and watch the way the background to the effect fits. Sometimes it may be preferable to keep the background running either side, especially if you can hear it behind the effect anyway. This care and attention is of course essential to all tracklaying. Common enough are the mistakes that arise from not examining a track carefully. For example, coughs, unwanted breathing and page turning are often forgotten on narration or voice-over even though it is easy enough to check for these things. On studio recordings it is not unusual for the mixer's announcements to end up being at least partially recorded and, even if they are eliminated in the final mix, it is very irritating for the mixer to have to close his pots (sound faders) completely between each section to avoid re-recording extraneous sound.

As each section of track is added, you should be aware of the need for positive sync reference points to avoid problems of re-synching especially when inserts are added to an already completed track. The ideal way is to quote on the sound track the last two digits of the code number opposite the frame on the picture. Use quick-drying felt-tip pen to avoid wax rubbing off on the oxide of the section which is going to be rolled tight against the mark. In this way the cutting copy need not be marked at all. Simply mark the sound frame in between the perforations. When the cutting copy is not coded, similar use can be made of key numbers if they are distinct enough for easy reference.

In all tracklaying you should follow the principle that no gaps should exist in sound of which the background atmosphere is a continuous complement to the visuals. If sections of the sync track have to be removed in the 'cleaning up' process always off-lay on another track a matching atmosphere or background overlapping with the sync sections, but *not* continuously across the existing sync. This allows the mixer to fade across with no noticeable change. With post-sync dialogue a continuous backing track may be valuable. Obviously, the availability of such background or buzz track depends upon the efficiency of the sound recordist.

It is tempting to attempt too much at once when laying sound tracks.

Remember that if you fill all the available heads on the synchronizer, there will be no spare to allow for lining up each section without removing the spacing or whatever already exists on the synchronizer. Even for experienced sound editors this can make the operation very complicated as sync marks have to be made each time something is removed; it is obviously more efficient to allow for a second run through to deal with the extra track.

The mechanics of tracklaying are not complicated but it is as well to follow a few simple rules:

1 Always cut the track in on the *left* of the synchronizer to avoid loss of sync in the material already laid.

2 Make all necessary sync marks before cutting so that nothing has to be re-adjusted after laying.

3 Review each section at sync speed to ensure that the desired effect is achieved – effects are pointless if the sound is not entirely appropriate.

4 Keep all spacer with the cell or base side against the heads so that there is no danger of emulsion rubbing off and causing build-up when re-recording.

5 Make end sync marks on the protective spacer at the end of a completed track common to all tracks and a similar mark on the picture.

6 Rewind each track 'sync' to those marks and check that it is still in sync at the front.

7 Run at normal speed with picture – preferably with another, relevant track to get a good indication of whether everything is working as expected.

8 Make sure there are no marks or accretions on the track surface and be careful to avoid bad joins.

9 Insert a frame of 1000 cycle tone opposite '3' on the leader of each track (some organizations use '4' instead of '3'). This sync plop is a more positive reference point than the sync mark, and will be used by the laboratory for lining up picture and sound for combined printing.

10 Ensure that the picture leader is the proper dubbing length. The standard is twelve 35 mm feet from the sync mark which is usually a cross or 'envelope'. If this is not adhered to all your footages will be wrong.

DUBBING CHARTS

It remains to tackle the dubbing chart. The formats vary in detail but the objective is always the same. Having laid your tracks efficiently it is imperative to convey the information that the mixer needs in a graphic and comprehensible form. It is to your advantage to make a rough chart as you lay each track. This avoids having to run all the tracks again for charting and allows you instantly to refer to other tracks already laid if you are in doubt about how to dovetail a certain element. It is fairly universal practice to dub to 35 mm footages, as 16 mm is too imprecise. Remember that one 35 mm foot is $\frac{2}{3}$ second at 24 frames, whereas one 16 mm foot is $1\frac{2}{3}$ seconds at 24 frames. Even so it is best to work to the nearest half a foot when charting, thus allowing accuracy of $\frac{1}{3}$ second for each cue. An essential part of the chart is picture cues. These need not list each change of shot, but commonsense and experience will tell you when it is useful to know the footage at a cut, dissolve or fade.

In drawing up the chart it is essential to be clear, consistent and accurate. The example demonstrates the simple code and signs that ensure the necessary communication.

DUBBING CHART	'FX' CUE SHEET				
Director *NICOLAS ROEG*		Production *BAD TIMING*			Reel 9
Action	FX 1	FX 2	FX 3	FX 4	FX 5
0 / 0 Street: morning	Traffic	9 Toot			
		20 / 12 Car door			
		27 / 29	Alarm		
		34 Toot			
90		90 / 37		88	90
Int. Flat	90 Traffic		107 / 101 Horse	Door 91	Cat
	135 Footsteps			116 Clock chime	116
			150 / 145 Alarm clock	134	165 W/T smash
	170		244 Radio	171 Baby	168
				252	
				283 Footsteps	W/T whistling
327 / 327 Office	Atmos.	327 337 Trolley	327	327	327
		354			

54 A simplified dubbing chart for part of one reel for the effects pre-mix on a feature film. Straight lines are used where effects are meant to cut in and out and sloping lines where they fade in and out. Each effect is identified and essential picture cues are given

THE MIX

Although the prime objective of tracklaying and mixing is to achieve a balanced combination of all sound reduced to one track, for convenience this is often arrived at through one or more intermediary steps. If there are more than four or five tracks to start with, mixing them down to one in a single operation is asking a lot of the mixer. It is therefore normal to go for one or more 'pre-mixes', usually balancing the tracks which contain similar elements. The most likely approach is to achieve a good balance of music and effects and to add all voice tracks in a later run-through. This music and effects mix, known as an M and E, is useful if foreign versions are contemplated, as it allows the replacement of voices by another language without having to re-mix from scratch. Of course if the music is the most important part of the film this should be added last, thus reducing the 'generations' gone through to a minimum.

Pre-mixes have one drawback. They commit you to an existing balance between those sound components when you are adding others. It takes considerable experience to predict the overall value of particular sounds when some of them are not being mixed at any given stage. Nor is it just a matter of levels. It is also very easy to assume that perspectives that seem right in isolation will still seem right when placed alongside other elements. A simple example is conversation on a dance floor with an orchestra audible in the background. We have all witnessed the film where the music is noticeably lowered in level when speech has to be heard, with a resultant loss of credibility. Here as in other such cases much can depend upon the approach used in the original recording. If the couple having the conversation have to raise their voices in the shooting situation then, although the balance may still be controllable because either the music was playback and/or the dialogue is post-sync, the final combined sound can be credibly mixed without undue emphasis on the discrepancy in levels.

We have naturally and quite rightly returned to the importance of having the proper attitude to sound from the outset – and that means from the time of writing the script. Unless the film-maker treats sound with the respect it deserves through all stages of production it will be undervalued and underexploited as the partner in the audio-visual medium of film. Ironically it is a lack of understanding of the functions of sound which more often than not means that films have too much of it. Inevitably we are reminded again of Bresson: 'The sound track created silence.' Indeed, discretion is the better part of tracklaying. There is no inherent value in having more elements in your track than you need. It is much more important to ensure that each sound has a proper function and is serving that function well.

7   The laboratory in post-production

The physical material that we call film is relatively delicate. The chemistry of the emulsion that film carries is not only fragile, it also depends upon the observation of fairly tight limitations to function effectively. It is perhaps appropriate that a device for capturing reality and the ability to reproduce it, should need precise handling. Indeed, before 'safety film' was invented the tendency of nitrate film virtually to self-destruct could almost be interpreted as natural justice against the arrogant and presumptuous desire of mankind to 'store' images of its own existence. Maybe fortunately, once we became blasé about film reality it only served to emphasize how marginal a part of our reality is actually conveyed by film. The mainsprings of our social and psychological existence are largely left untouched by the medium, perhaps because we are predominantly concerned with the 'reality' that is on the surface. Just as 'beauty is skin deep' so 'film reality is emulsion deep'.

Nevertheless this fragile material is loaded into cameras, exposed, unloaded, sent to the laboratory and processed in the belief that if certain guidelines are followed carefully an acceptable result will be obtained. Further, the print obtained from the processed material is edited in the belief that after the negative or master is matched to it the laboratory can reproduce, or even improve on, the result seen in the rushes. Bearing in mind that cinematography as applied to the art of movie making is not meant to be a science, and that no cameraman worth his salt is looking for mere 'photographic' efficiency, it is fairly surprising that the final result is often very close to that desired by the director, editor and cameraman.

There are those who wish that film stocks and camera lenses could have a performance equivalent to the optic nerve. That would release us from a preoccupation with trying to 'match' reality. It is of course the lack of desire to do this which is one of the signs that a film-maker should be taken seriously – although avoidance of concern with reproducing the surface reality may not necessarily be anything but laziness or pretension. However, since many of my favourite movies were made in black-and-white in the standard Academy aspect ratio, I am not about to argue that closer facsimiles of 'reality' are bound to lead to better films.

Unfortunately the search for better emulsions, faster lenses, more efficient processing and a greater degree of standardization leads to deplorable tendencies which the laboratories are forced to follow. Both Technicolor's abandoning of the dye-transfer system of printing and the running down of black-and-white processing, are examples of industrial practice restricting an art form in the service of efficiency and standardization.

What needs emphasizing is that film-makers *must* familiarize themselves sufficiently with what the laboratory does and has to offer, to be able to take maximum advantage of the high degree of expertise available there. The best laboratory technicians have always desired to and been able to contribute much to films beyond the mere slavish interpretation of how your material matches up to some abstract standard.

So how can you use this expertise to its maximum? Unfortunately, we are easily and early socialized into the wrong attitude by the chemist shop routine. We become used to providing minimal information in our first encounters with stills processing. Asked such questions as: 'en-prints or enlargements?', 'glossy or matte?' by a teenage assistant more used to selling hair lacquer and razor blades does not prepare us for the possibility that the professional film laboratory can supply a profoundly more sophisticated service if we establish a higher level of communication.

THE 'CONTACT'

It is not accidental that the person most important to a film-maker at the laboratory is called the 'contact'. Usually there is a particular person who co-ordinates rushes and it is imperative that you make contact with him or her *before* starting to shoot. Informing the rushes person of your schedule, arrangements for sending in the exposed material and return of the rush print, and of any particular problems you foresee, can make a great deal of difference to the smoothness of this part of the operation. If, during shooting, there are doubts raised about the rushes, then instant contact must be made to ascertain if there is a problem and whether it is irredeemably built into the negative or if the laboratory can eliminate it for the purpose of later printing. I have already discussed this fully (see p. 61) but the importance of vigilance and quick action bears restating.

Once the film is shot, responsibility for it almost invariably passes to the post-production contact who will see it through to at least the first acceptable show or release print. Subsequent copies are often handled by another person. This way liaison for reprints, opticals, titles, negative cutting, grading and printing are funnelled through the same individual. At any given point in the process it is difficult to resist the desire to talk directly to whoever is handling a particular aspect – this should always be possible, but to avoid confusion it is obviously best to make any arrangements through that one contact. It is also imperative that you avoid splitting responsibility for liaising with the laboratory between too many people. If director, editor, assistant editor and even cameraman are giving conflicting information and instructions, the contact will not know whom to satisfy or even to whom to refer. So delegation of particular jobs in relation to the laboratory must be carefully handled.

REPRINTS AND DUPLICATION

The first likely requirements during cutting are reprints and duplication of stock or library footage, the latter only on compilation films or where a specific shot could not be obtained in the material shot especially for the film. Reprints may be required because the editor and/or director is not happy with the rush print and would like to confirm that a section is usable. They may also be necessary if footage is damaged during editing and must be replaced in the cutting copy to confirm the effectiveness of a sequence. For the laboratory to supply such reprints it is essential to give them the key numbers of the start and end of the section required and also, if possible, the camera-sheet number, the roll number and shooting date. Not all this information may be necessary but, as with all requests to the laboratory, it is better to give too much data than too little. You may be able to facilitate speedy supply by telephoning a request, but it will always be best to back it up with a written order. So a reprint order might read:

PLEASE SUPPLY: 'TITLE'
    16 mm COLOUR CORRECTED RUSH PRINT OF SECTION BK66869–943
    FROM EASTMANCOLOR NEGATIVE IN YOUR POSSESSION
    CAMERA SHEET: 04672
    SHOOTING DATE: 8 JUNE 1979
    ROLL NUMBER: 15

As with all orders it is as well to print in BLOCK CAPITALS the essential information. Note that the request is for *colour corrected* rush print. This is to help gauge the best possible result from the negative. You may well add special instructions, e.g., MATERIAL SHOT IN LOW LIGHT CONDITIONS – PLEASE PRINT UP FOR MAXIMUM DETAIL, or RUSH PRINT SHOWS NEGATIVE SCRATCHES PLEASE TREAT BEFORE PRINTING.

At this point I should sound a note of warning. Reprints are expensive, there is usually a minimum charge and in any case it is technically difficult for the laboratory to supply less than 50 feet. Where you merely desire to check on questionable material, it may be best to ask the contact to get the section in question examined and reported on. It is usually possible to find out whether scratches can be removed or polished out without going to the expense of a reprint. If you are forced to work in black-and-white on a colour film it is sometimes essential to have sections in colour to check on such things as exposure, focus and fogging. You should also bear in mind that every time the negative is handled there is some risk of damage or accretion of 'sparkle' (dirt) – not because laboratories are careless but merely because film is a fragile material. So always convince yourself that your reprint is essential.

Duplicating from library or stock footage has other problems. You must first be certain of the type of master material that is being 'duped'. It may be negative or reversal, it may be a master print. The gauge may be 35 mm or 16 mm. If it is 35 mm the format may be other than Academy. Always remember that your objective is to obtain a negative or master and a rush print that will conform with your other material. The source of the stock footage will tell you in what form the laboratory can supply the shots you want duped, and you must be sure that your requirements are clear.

The most common complication in duping happens when you have shot material on negative and need stock shots from reversal material. The geometry is reversed between a contact print from negative and reversal masters or camera originals, so to see the image the right way round a contact print from negative is correct with the emulsion to the observer, whereas with reversal original the base is on the side of the observer. So an internegative made from a reversal original will be unusable for intercutting.

The shorthand method of referring to emulsion position is 'A' wind and 'B' wind. A wind refers to material that is correct when the *emulsion* is towards the observer and B wind refers to material that is correct when the *base* is towards the observer. So when ordering dupes it is best to specify the wind required, especially if you are mixing negative and reversal. Remember that both original negative and reversal original are B wind but internegative from reversal original is A wind.

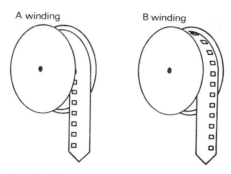

A winding   B winding

55 In A winding the film is correct when the emulsion is towards the observer; in B winding it is correct when the emulsion is away from the observer

This necessity to make all your material conform to the same geometry also applies to optical sound tracks, so a track for original negative or reversal must be B wind. If, however, your picture is an internegative the track must be A wind. If you have any doubts it is essential either to specify on the order to what your duplicate must conform, or to ask the laboratory for clarification.

The danger is that it is possible to join together material which has contrary geometry and even to be unaware that you have different emulsion positions at a cut. The loss of focus is marginal enough to be hardly discernible on an editing machine and you may therefore only become aware of the problem when the cutting copy is sent to the negative cutters. It can be a real disaster if the material you have duped from is hard to obtain again for re-duping when there may be pressure on completing the film – so get it right first time!

OPTICALS

Apart from reprints and duping there may be little contact between cutting room and laboratory before the fine cut is completed. The one important exception is the need for opticals. Because A and B printing allows for dissolves and fades to be part of the final printing process it is quite common for the only optical requirement to be the superimposition of titles. You may decide to go for straight titles without superimposition, partly because of cost and partly because it is no longer believed that the mere existence of elaborate title sequences has anything to do with the quality of the film itself. If, however, superimpositions are desired, several factors must be remembered. The shots for title overlay should be carefully considered before shooting starts, since a suitable background is essential:

1   The shots should be steady to avoid appearance of 'jiggle'.
2   They should be low key if the lettering is to be the normal white (and high key if titles are black).
3   You should decide in advance where in the frame the titles will be positioned, as no action or relevant background detail should be obscured by the titles. However, too much lettering will either be cramped if restricted to a small part of the frame or require a long period of superimposition.
4   Avoid wide angle or shots where there is distortion of straight lines, either horizontal or vertical.
5   Remember that the cost of your optical superimposition is related to the *total* length of the shot used as background, and *not* to the length of the title overlay itself. It is possible to cut in a dupe of just the section with the title but the result will almost certainly be unsatisfactory as the change to and from the section duped will not match the original quality.

So the ideal title background is static, on a tripod, using say a 50 mm lens, of a relatively dark subject (for white titles) that does not include too much fussy detail.

You may, of course, opt for a roller caption instead of static titles – this demands accurate timing to ensure that you allow sufficient length in the shooting of the background shot. Whether the titles are static or rolling (or even if they are straight) several rules must be observed:

1   The titles must be steady and accurately positioned.
2   They must be shot on high contrast stock and properly exposed, otherwise they will 'bleed'.
3   They must not be too tight to the edges of frame (for television the safe area is particularly restricted).
4   The lettering should not be too fussy or too small – remember that if the type face is not easy to read in isolation it will be even harder when superimposed.

When you have the material for optical superimposition, the order to the laboratory must be very carefully prepared. Some laboratories will supply special order forms for this purpose, but in any case the information they require is always similar. Ideally you should submit both a written breakdown and a cutting-copy guide.

The breakdown needs to be something like this:

START BACKGROUND DUPE AT $\boxed{\text{AC}}$ 241076 − 5 frames.
START 16 frame fade in of 'MAIN TITLE' at AC 2410 $\boxed{81}$ + 6 frames.
END 16 frame fade out of 'MAIN TITLE' at AC 2410 $\boxed{94}$ + 17 frames.
END BACKGROUND DUPE AT AC 2411 $\boxed{07}$ + 12 frames.

The boxed letters and numbers, e.g. $\boxed{\text{AC}}$ or $\boxed{81}$, refer to the particular frame from which the calculation is made. The plus or minus frames from this point take you to the actual frame for the desired effect to start or finish. If this frame is actually numbered you should write it thus: $\boxed{\text{AC}}$ 241076 ± 0 frames.

It is possible to use only plus signs, which is visually clearer, but if you are submitting a cutting-copy guide it makes sense to refer only to frames that are in that guide. Thus, in the example above, START BACKGROUND

DUPE AT $\boxed{\text{AC}}$ 241076 − 5 frames, is better than AC 2410 $\boxed{75}$ + 13 frames, as that number will not occur in the guide.

The ordering of dissolves or other transitional effects is similar except that the centre point must be referred to. Thus, after noting the starting frame of the dupe, you must list the frames immediately each side of the middle of the effect (i.e. at the cut point in the cutting copy), e.g.

CENTRE of 32 frame dissolve at $\begin{array}{l}\text{DB } 1035 \boxed{68} + 2 \text{ frames} \\ \boxed{\text{XY}}\ 794812 - 10 \text{ frames}\end{array}$

and follow this with the end frame of the second shot.

To make a cutting-copy guide you remove the relevant background shot(s) from the work print and show the desired effects with standard markings. Perhaps the ideal form in which to supply such a guide is to insert white spacer in the synchronizer alongside the background shots and to mark up with felt-tip pen the equivalent effects and title information as appropriate. A simple superimposition would look like this:

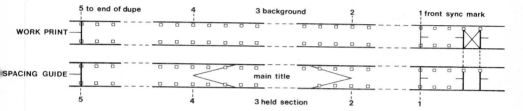

The above represents in schematic form: the start of the dupe (1); the point at which the superimposed title fades in over a specified number of frames from (2); the title is held for a specified number of frames (3); then faded out over a specified number of frames to (4); the background continues to its own cut point (5). The same sort of guide can be used for a whole series of superimpositions or indeed for other forms of optical. If opticals are ordered while you are still cutting, always insert the equivalent length of spacing to replace shots removed as guides.

As I said above, dissolves are obtainable in A and B printing so they are not normally required as opticals. However, such A and B effects are only available at specified length, usually the following:

8 frames	=	$\frac{1}{3}$ second	(at 24 frames)
16 frames	=	$\frac{2}{3}$ second	,,
24 frames	=	1 second	,,
32 frames	=	$1\frac{1}{3}$ seconds	,,
48 frames	=	2 seconds	,,
64 frames	=	$2\frac{2}{3}$ seconds	,,
96 frames	=	4 seconds	,,

There is one further limitation: such dissolves must be a certain number of frames apart since the printer cannot be cued instantaneously. It is as well to check with your laboratory if you suspect that the effects you want might be too close together. The minimum is at least 12 frames between the end of one dissolve and the start of the next, but it may be more.

Remember that all effects that demand an overlap of shots require you to be certain that the extra frames of each shot concerned are usable. In the cutting copy these overlap frames do not exist and, unless you check as you cut, it is imperative to look at the front or end trim when marking up for such effects.

The optical department is a source of much magic which results directly from the fact that film is made up of static images. The frame can be stopped or frozen; you can speed up the action or slow it down; blow up the frame, making a close-up out of a medium shot; reverse the action; combine different actions; diffuse the image; even superimpose rain or fog! However, because obtaining these effects is labour-intensive and demands special film stock, the cost is very high. Unless you are prepared to budget in advance for such things, they must be a last resort and normally used only because a particular dramatic effect is unobtainable in any other way or because you are convinced that the optical in question is the best way of achieving that effect.

I am tending in this chapter to consider things on a purely technical level, but we should not forget that everything the laboratory contributes to the film is in the service of its style and content. If we are reduced to considering opticals, for example, as abstract effects, we have lost touch with the life of the film. Consider too for a moment why we should augment the language of a film with dissolves, fades and other opticals. It used to be true to assume that the dissolve merely conveyed a passage of time and that a fade out was taken to mean the end of a scene and perhaps a more emphatic time lapse, combined sometimes with a change of location. We are now more willing to accept such changes of time and place on a simple cut, preferring perhaps to develop the way pacing and rhythm convey the logic of the narrative. This has released optical effects for a wider range of uses. Dissolving two shots, for instance, can emphasize connections between places and people that have their own continuum within the structure of the narrative. Such juxtapositions allow the film-maker to convey to the audience the thoughts of characters and the film-maker's own attitude to the drama, without the need for words. So a dancer sitting alone in the quiet of her dressing room is cued into the thought and emotion of a ballet by the music seeping into her, and therefore into our consciousness, so that the dissolve through to an earlier performance serves to emphasize and particularize that sensation. In this case the dissolve is an alternative to a straight cut and would be chosen as much because of the mood of the piece as out of consideration of the time/space relationship between the two scenes.

Sound is always an important element in the use of opticals and indeed can often be substituted for dissolves or fades. The effect of fading sound to a cut is sometimes more interesting than the visual equivalent. Of course, it is imperative to co-ordinate the use of opticals with the matching sound effects during the mixing of the film – it is no good having a smooth visual transition if the sound is an abrupt cut.

The one drawback of A and B opticals is that you do not see them until you receive an answer print from the cut negative. So you must be as certain as possible that the dissolves and fades will work as expected, especially in terms of the length you decide upon. If possible, insert both shots being dissolved in the gate of your editing machine. As long as neither shot is too dense you can get an indication of how the two shots will 'mesh'. Unless the density of both shots is very similar one or other will dominate the dissolve – a darker shot loses effectiveness quicker and a lighter shot is apparent sooner. You should also be very vigilant about movement and composition during the passage of dissolves. An awkward movement that starts during a dissolve is disconcerting and if, for instance, you are dissolving one face through to another face the positioning in frame will affect the design of the superimposed section.

One last point about fades – it is not a rigid rule that a fade out and fade in should always be used together. If, for instance, you want to leave a scene quietly but hit the next scene abruptly, there is nothing to stop you fading out and cutting in. Indeed it is possible to fade out, hold on black for a beat or two then cut in. The reverse can also be effective – cutting to black and fading up after a pause.

Incorporating effects demands as much thought as each cut you make. Never assume that a particular junction of shots requires the use of an optical because of some hidebound logic of film grammar. Maybe the juxtaposition is wrong and you have perhaps wasted the opportunity of a pause or the insertion of an extra shot. It is sometimes the case, on the other hand, that both shots have been allowed to die at the cut, and should be shortened to make a more dynamic confluence. For the fact is that dissolves are often the easy way out of a problem caused by ineffective shooting. This is always a negative reason for using opticals, so be honest with yourself every time the idea of using such effects comes into your head!

NEGATIVE AND ORIGINAL CUTTING

Once cutting has been completed the cutting copy must be prepared for the negative cutters. To avoid confusion and the possibility of mistakes it must be carefully examined and marked clearly with standard indications that instruct the negative cutter of particular requirements. Each reel must have a standard leader to allow for lace up in projection, synchronization, protection from damage and identification – the last consisting of clear title and roll number markings on opaque leader or spacing. The standard markings used during cutting have already been described in full (see p. 72). Those that must be retained at this stage are the marks indicating the unintended splice, build-up, extension, dissolve and fade.

All these must be clear and precise and any other marks not relevant to the negative cutter should be removed to avoid misinterpretation. You may have plastered the cutting copy with sync marks, cue marks for post-synchronization and any number of now irrelevant accretions. These must be excised before sending off the cutting copy. Remember also to add protective leader to the end of each reel, clearly marked so that it can be identified immediately even if tail out.

The most common form of negative cutting on 16 mm is chequerboard. The joins are eliminated during printing by putting each shot on alternate rolls and lapping black spacer on the roll which is without a shot at any given point. This is an extension of A and B rolling where alternate rolls are used only when a fade or dissolve is required. It is a technique used because the 16 mm frame line is far too narrow to allow for a join overlap. Some laboratories use an alternative to chequerboard to eliminate joins: 'zero cut' or auto-splice deletion which incorporates an overlap of frames at each cut either on two rolls as in A and B or in a single roll. A special shutter device is used to eliminate the extra frames and, although there may be a one-frame overlap of images at the cut, no join will be visible. If you are ordering chequerboard negative cutting the laboratory in question will inform you if they offer an alternative method.

Always remember that at least three or four frames are lost at each cut during negative cutting. Since tape joiners make it possible to cut without losing frames, this must be borne in mind especially when using a shot twice. Otherwise there will be no way of matching your cutting copy short of re-synchronizing and/or cutting the sound track.

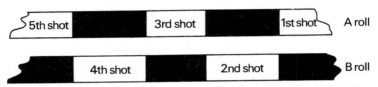

56 A and B roll chequerboard assembly. This method also allows for the incorporation of dissolves and fades in the printing

GRADING AND PRINTING

Once the negative has been cut to match your cutting copy the film is ready to be graded. Although your rush prints may have been largely acceptable in their rendition of the shot material, grading has to be related to matching the film shot by shot as cut. If, for instance, the reverse angles that you have intercut were not matched in their respective lighting set-ups, the discrepancy will be dramatized by cutting them together. It is irrelevant that shots may have looked all right in the rushes: grading is not a process of looking for the ideal rendering of each shot but of achieving an acceptable balance throughout each sequence and indeed throughout the whole film.

At the first stage of grading the procedure will vary depending upon your particular laboratory. Modern equipment allows for analysis of the cut negative by electronically 'reverse-phasing' the image so that it is seen as positive. The most sophisticated machinery of this kind can run both A and B rolls simultaneously and the cutting copy can be projected as a reference. The value of running the cutting copy is partly to compensate for the shortcomings of an electronic reading of a photographic image. As the grader watches the monitor, he can instantly rebalance the colour by reducing or increasing the amount of yellow, cyan and magenta components, i.e. the negative equivalents of the three primary colours. He will make extensive notes for the grading of the print, but basically each shot will end up with three numbers alongside it in his list, referring to the printer values for the three primary colour components.

It is natural for director and editor to wish to consult with the grader at this stage, at least to point out any shots or sequences that they feel need abnormal treatment. Ideally, if a viewing of the cutting copy and/or a session on the analyser can take place, it will allow the film-makers the opportunity to pre-empt any mistaken interpretations of colour and density. It will also allow the grader the chance to demonstrate what is possible and what limitations exist with regard to 'correction' of the image. However, such discussions depend upon the availability of time and facilities, both of which are often at a premium at the laboratory. Even so, the least that must be done before any prints are struck is for the editor to supply careful annotations of all potential problem areas in the film so that the grader is not working totally abstracted from the 'feel' of the film.

Even with thorough and exhaustive consultation it is unlikely that the first attempt or 'answer print' will be entirely satisfactory, and further corrections will then be made before another print is struck. When checking the answer print, always project it under optimum conditions, otherwise the colour balance and overall density will be misrepresented. Do not be surprised to find that there is a discernible variation between different projectors. The intensity of the lamp and its age, the lens on the projector, the length of 'throw' to the screen, the screen surface and the degree of darkness in the viewing room will all affect the appearance of the image and must be taken into account when estimating the quality of the print.

When this first attempt is being viewed, several other checks must be made in addition to those of colour balance and overall density:

1 Is the print clean or has the negative acquired an unacceptable degree of 'sparkle' or dirt during handling?
2 Are there any scratches which need treating? Watch especially for dirt and scratches at the beginning and end of reels and also at joins.

57 The Hazeltine analyser for grading allows for electronic viewing of negative as positive and independent correction of the three primary colours

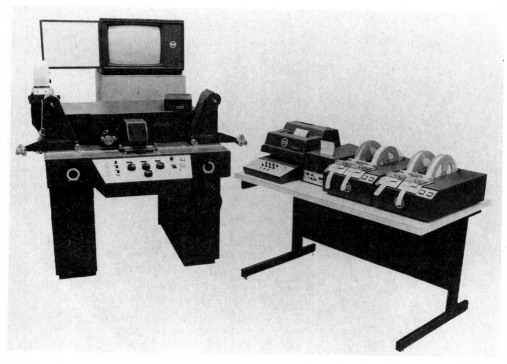

3   Is the sound track of acceptable quality and in sync with the picture?
    You will invariably be disappointed with a 16mm optical track, but
    the inevitable degradation compared with the master magnetic
    should only be marginal and another transfer should be ordered if it
    is totally unsatisfactory.

4   Are the A and B opticals what you expected? Watch for jumps in
    fades and dissolves which may result from a fault in the cueing
    device. If dissolves or fades do not produce the required effect they
    can be shortened or eliminated, but remember any alterations to the
    cueing of the print will mean treating the next attempt as a new
    answer print at a higher cost than if it is termed a show copy or
    release print.

Assuming that no substantial problems exist with the answer print
there should now be further consultation with the grader to correct the
unsatisfactory shots. Viewing the answer print with the grader is the best
method of communicating requests for modifications, since you can
discuss and clarify points which may be too subtle to reduce to a few
words on paper. In addition, this is probably the first time he has heard
the sound track and thus can get a proper sense of the atmosphere of the
film. Grading is meant to complement the mood and this can only be
conveyed when picture and sound are together.

If, however, you are reduced to a written report then the easiest system
is to insert numbered pieces of paper in the print and to list your
comments correspondingly. Perhaps the hardest part of communicating
desired grading corrections is to use a language or form of words that are
least open to misinterpretation. You will mostly be dealing with pairs of
words that suggest a range between some form of extremes. Do not be
tempted to write an essay about the psychology or philosophy of the film
as there is no way this can be translated into printer lights by the grader.
The following is the kind of information he will appreciate:

1   Scenes are: too dark/too light
              high contrast/low contrast
              too saturated/de-saturated (refers to colour intensity)
              too warm/too cold

2   You can refer to colour bias that you want emphasized or removed.

3   Perhaps the best method is to refer to a particular shot in a sequence
    as being the one to grade to. This can be done either in reference to
    the cutting copy or, if appropriate, the answer print. For example, a
    note saying 'Grade all shots in sequence between papers as per second
    shot (W/S dining room)', allows the grader the best possible chance
    of getting it right.

Grading can never compensate for an unsatisfactory negative. If you
use material that is under- or over-exposed or insert a shot that contains
the wrong colour balance compared to the rest of the sequence, you are
taking a considerable risk. Recognizing such limitations is an inevitable
part of being an editor and you should always be ready to weigh the
value of a shot against its photographic shortcomings. A 'good' negative,
that is, one that has received optimum exposure, is the only guarantee of
flexibility in grading. If you have congratulated yourself on obtaining an
incredible shot on the end of a 16mm zoom with the lens wide open you

must be prepared to live with poor resolution and colour balance. Indeed, it cannot be emphasized too strongly that a lack of meticulous vetting of your cutting copy with grading potential in mind will inevitably lead to problems in the print. There must be a proper screening of the cutting copy before sending it to the laboratory for negative cutting. Often the odd frame that is fogged or damaged will escape your attention under the less than perfect conditions of the editing machine, and this is especially true at the beginning and end of shots. A dark rush print can hide embarrassing detail which will be made apparent when graded up. Never assume that familiarity with your material is the same as being aware of every detail.

Orders for negative cutting and printing must be as precise as those we discussed earlier for opticals. Never assume that information can be taken for granted. Always mention the following:

1 Title
2 Gauge
3 Original stock
4 What you are sending with the order
5 What is held by the laboratory
6 Your requirements

Every order describes one or more processes. In each case you are asking for a product to be supplied from existing raw material. Thus an order for negative cutting should read:

TITLE (1)

Please supply 16mm (2) chequerboard negative cutting (6) from Eastmancolor negative (3) in your possession (5) to match cutting copy herewith (4). Please hold for printing instructions.

To obtain the optical track the order should state:

TITLE (1)

Please supply 16mm (2) optical sound track (6) from 16mm magnetic master herewith (4). Track should be B wind to match Eastmancolor negative (3) in your possession (5). Sync plop on 3 of leader. Please hold developed negative for combined printing – order to follow.

For grading and printing you should state:

TITLE (1)

Please grade (6) 16mm Eastmancolor cut negative (3) in your possession (5) as discussed, and with reference to notes herewith (4), and make combined answer print (6) with optical sound track (plop on 3 of leader) advancing for printing sync, from optical sound negative in your possession (5). Please send print to the cutting room (address).

If you are synchronizing your sound track for printing you must know that the number of frames the sound track is advanced is as follows:

35 mm optical — 20 frames.
16 mm optical — 26 frames.
16 mm magnetic stripe — 28 frames.

You must then inform the laboratory that you are supplying the track in PRINTING SYNC.

With regard to 16 mm magnetic stripe you should remember that while the quality can be better than 16 mm optical it does restrict the showing of such prints to those projectors which have a magnetic replay head. When ordering 16 mm stripe prints you must request that after making the mute print the laboratory should apply the stripe and transfer from the magnetic master on to the stripe again in printing sync with reference to the sync plop that you specify.

One further point about combined printing. If your film is being printed in more than one reel, which is normal on 35 mm for anything over 20 minutes and on 16 mm for anything over 50 minutes (although in the latter case each reel may be considerably shorter), you must specify the need for the recording of a sound overlap on the end of the first reel and any subsequent reels, including the penultimate one. This is to compensate for the fact that, when two reels are joined together, the sound advance on the second is cut off and must therefore appear on the end of the first one. So, in terms of 16 mm optical, the first 26 frames of reel 2 sound must appear alongside the last 26 frames of reel 1 picture. This is not necessary if it is intended *always* to run the film with the reels separate.

If, however, you run the film in separate reels then each reel that is not the last must be cued for projection change-over. This can be done by the laboratory if requested, but otherwise you need the use of a cue-dot marker. This device will apply a mark, which is normally circular, to four successive frames at two separate points near the end of the reel. These appear in the top right-hand corner of the frame, the first cue for 'striking up' the second projector and the second for the actual change-over. Since 16 mm projectors can usually take up to 2000 feet of film it is now unusual to need cue dots on that gauge. However, 35 mm films of over 20 minutes would normally require at least one change-over. When applying cue dots you must know the number of frames from the end that they should appear (see Glossary). The easiest way is to mark up in the synchronizer, preferably with the use of a template already prepared on a length of spacer.

DUPLICATING THE MASTER

Once you have obtained an acceptable show copy or release print of the film there remains little for you as the editor to do. If it is expected that a considerable number of prints will be needed then you have to consider whether it is worth the expense of making a duplicate master from your negative to protect the original. As a general rule it is unwise to expect to obtain more than five prints without the danger of damage to the negative. Each time it is handled you run the risk of damage in the form of scratches or blemishes and not all marks can be successfully removed by cleaning and polishing. In any case you should specify that the negative must be cleaned whenever reordering after the initial prints.

Deciding to make a protection dupe is obviously better done early, otherwise you are shutting the door after the horse has bolted. These days there are two basic systems of duplicating from colour material. One is the C.R.I. or Colour Reversal Intermediate, which has the advantage of being one process. The other is to go through interpositive and internegative, which has the drawback of being two stages, but once you have a satisfactory interpositive, successive internegatives can be made from it and you are doubly protected from having to touch the original cut negative.

STORAGE AND RETENTION OF THE MASTER

Do not forget that arrangements must be made for storage of your master material. The cut negative and sound master will be held by the laboratory for a considerable time after completion. You should also hang on to the magnetic track master and any music and effects track that exists. The dubbing tracks and charts and the cutting copy should be retained until you are absolutely certain that no alternative versions of the film will be made. The rush print trims and magnetic track trims can usually be junked fairly soon, but the original $\frac{1}{4}$-in. tapes should be kept as protection. Any material that is retained should be stored under conditions that inhibit the natural process of deterioration, i.e. where temperature and humidity are neither too high, nor too low nor tend to fluctuate widely. Every can and box should be clearly labelled and properly secured.

So this is the end of the line. There is no more for the editor to do, except for certain returns and records required by the production office (see Appendix, p. 135).

8 Film editing and the future: film or video?

The techniques and craft described in this book have assumed the existing state of technology in the cutting room. The basic methods of film editing have remained substantially the same for many years, and the way films have been conceived and shot has also assumed the way editing functions. In terms of dramatic film this has included the assumptions of one camera, breaking down each scene into shots and the ability to shoot out of script order.

In the last thirty years however, the multi-camera, continuous and chronological approach to videotaping has established a sister medium. Until recently the two methods have remained largely discrete – the use of film sequences in video programmes is still an uneasy marriage. However, many factors have influenced the choice between them. Some of these factors have been economic. Film is a wasteful medium. The raw material is not reusable and about ten times the amount of film is consumed than eventually ends up on the screen – a profligate use of expensive material. Film is also labour- and time-intensive. Videotape, on the other hand, is reusable and with the incorporation of multi-camera techniques on a tight schedule many economies can be made.

Recent developments have now blurred the edges between tape and film to a degree that their potential effect on how the editing phase is handled can no longer be ignored. Firstly, the video camera is fast approaching the flexibility of the film camera and, secondly, video editing has leap-frogged film cutting in its sophistication and efficiency. However, all this might have far less effect on the editing process than one would imagine. For it is possible to argue that the traditional way of shooting film is still the best method to apply to videotaping if, in the editing, the tape can be treated as if it were film. It is also patently obvious that the single-camera, shot-by-shot technique still offers the most flexibility in editing. It is also the method that encourages the use of the most sophisticated visual language and the retention of those aesthetic advantages which are related to control over lighting and other aspects of staging inhibited by the use of multi-cameras.

What is likely to change, however, is the extent to which even film material will continue to be *cut* on film. Consider that film can be transferred to a videotape positive by reverse-phasing the developed negative, thus eliminating the need for printing a cutting copy. Consider further that all this videotape can be logged by computer. Add to this the ability with video to search for and find any particular section in seconds and the fact that video allows you to preview a cut before you make it and to programme alternatives instantly, and editing on film becomes the equivalent of a cottage industry compared with the production line which video offers.

However, that analogy is carefully chosen. Production lines are fast becoming robot-operated. It is not simply reactionary to sound a warning

58 This composite picture shows a CMX Video Display Unit in the foreground, an effects generator (right) and replay and recording machines in the background

about the way in which video editing is applied: I have dwelt long and hard on the function of pace and rhythm in cutting and I believe that there is also an inherent value in the way film editing inhibits the pace at which decisions are taken and imposes its own rhythm on the editor.

It would be deceptive of me to imply that everyone is as wary as this of the dangers of embracing electronic editing techniques. Dede Allen has said: '[Film] editing is a process where your mind and your concept work much faster than the techniques of being able to fulfil it. . . . Everything that is done technically is always much slower than the way you'd like to see it come, which is why the electronic system is going to be so great when it becomes economically feasible.' (*Wide Angle*, vol 2, no. 1, 1977.) However, it must be borne in mind that she is speaking from the standpoint of someone who has learned her craft in the traditional way and, in any case, she is in favour of electronic techniques as an aid to film editing rather than as a substitute. It is likely that there is a risk of never learning the film editor's craft if the beginner is initiated into the magic through instant video techniques. Remember what happened to the sorcerer's apprentice.

What is so disconcerting is the appearance of the technology. Video-editing desks make the traditional film-cutting machines look very primitive by comparison. The combination of myriad monitors, a visual display unit and keyboards with dozens of buttons seems to suggest that there is no argument as to which method offers the most sophisticated and complex system (as you can see from the illustration). However, apart from special effects and instant multiple-image capability, the fact remains that the basic function of editing is the same whatever the technology. A good and effective juxtaposition, when the aim is to serve the purpose of telling a story or representing events, is still best achieved by finding the right cut and combination of cuts. As soon as you lose sight of this objective the technology will take over. At any given time editing must be concerned with finding one particular conjunction of images and anything which blurs this process is inherently dangerous. For familiarization with your material is far more than impressing on your consciousness the nature of the alternative visuals for each scene. Each of those images carries an emotional charge, a psychological force, which informs the way it can interact with other material. Instant accessibility and, indeed, simultaneous display of these alternatives, carry with them the danger of reacting only to the surface impact. Editing is a process of revealing, of using the power of controlling expectations and motivating a response to *each next image*. It is this use of a hidden power that allows the editor to make creative use of his craft. Complex video editing, it seems to me, is inclined to close off this essential mental process by making the alternatives too visible.

There is another aspect of the tape versus film controversy that must be borne in mind. Peck Prior, then head of Technicolor Cinema Division, was quoted in *American Cinemeditor* (Winter 1976/77) as saying: 'The physical pleasure of film is difficult to translate to videotape. Do you remember your first film experience? Alone with film: cutting it, handling it, wrapped up in it – tape doesn't have that. It has another kind of feeling – there is less than meets the eye to knowing it too.'

The physical process of handling the film as you make and alter decisions about how to cut it is an integral part of the way you relate to that material. There is no doubt in my mind that the development of the language of film editing thus far has depended as much as anything on this physical relationship with the recorded images. Even if you wish to argue that to a degree this has encouraged adherence to a sterile convention, it still remains true that handling film and especially the process of marking up a cut and splicing two sections together somehow determines the way you relate to making those decisions.

Let us compare the difference between video and film to that between the techniques of the two painters Canaletto and Turner. Canaletto, by using the *camera obscura*, was able to arrive at what appears to be a precise representation of his scene with utmost facility. Turner, on the other hand, made sketches of a scene and later, sometimes after many years, applied his individual interpretation to the original experience without feeling tied to the precise detail of the 'reality'. Film editing is never quite on that plane of creativity, but just as I would argue that Canaletto's work was in the realm of charming but essentially dead images and that Turner communicated the work of a fine imagination, so I would claim that the traditional way film editing is approached encourages a vital contribution to the end product that sophisticated electronic techniques mitigate against. The validity of this attitude will only be tested in the way the practices are applied in the future, but so many areas of creativity have succumbed to the criterion of immediacy and to concepts divorced from the experience that the artefacts represents, that it is hard to believe that video can be used in a way that is as disciplined and creative as film.

The area that even now remains virtually untouched by electronic techniques is the feature film for the cinema. Not only is the quality of 35 mm film still light years ahead of the video image but the size of the image in the cinema demands that quality. This gulf is emphasized by such factors as the variations in shape of the image available with film and the depth of field available with 35 mm prime lenses. Furthermore, all I have argued about the way editing functions on film is especially true of the feature film. Its style and form are not, it would seem, encompassable in the electronic mode.

Maybe feature films will sometimes be shown from videotape in the future, but the present state of video projection on any screen big enough to be suitable for cinema demonstrates an unacceptable lack of brightness, contrast and resolution (see Appendix 'B2', in A.C.T.T. Annual Report, 1979/80, 61–3). Even if this is substantially improved it is difficult to see feature films being made on tape for some time to come. It is much more likely that 16 mm, perhaps in the super 16 mm format, will become the gauge for some of the lower budget end of production.

One of the most seductive aspects of video editing is the availability of instant effects which are both more flexible and far less expensive than on film. These effects include freeze-framing, slow motion, mirror image, zooming, filters, drop shadow and many kinds of transition from shot to shot.

Meanwhile, film is fighting back. Aaton, the camera people, have developed a system which allows for a number reference to be applied to the film stock at the time of exposure and also to transpose a corresponding reference to the magnetic track when transferring from the ¼-in. tape. By thus removing the need for clapperboards and numbering an instant sync and retrieval reference is supplied. As part of the technology a cross-reference continuity/shot-listing device is also available. The incorporation of a system like this into normal film production would obviously reinforce the feasibility of film as a convenient medium in competition with videotape.

In the final analysis, whether we use videotape or film, the basic language is the same. It is obviously of great value to use the instant replay on video to learn the rudiments of the language and no film editor should ignore the learning potential available through tape. The quicker you become aware of the pitfalls and the solutions in editing situations the better. If electronic techniques can give you access to an alternative method of understanding the right approach to editing, this opportunity should be grasped with both hands.

In this book I have attempted to convey something of the elements which make film editing so particular. It has to do with the ambience in the cutting room, the equipment you work on, the relationship between director and editor and, more than anything else, the degree to which the conception of the film takes into account the potential and expected contribution that editing can make. The thought that I must leave you with is the same as that with which I began this book: editing should never be undertaken as if it were emergency surgery after the traumas and accidents of shooting. It is tempting for editors to feel that they can save movies; this is never true: there has to be potential in the footage for editing to contribute anything.

One last thought: the temptation to behave as if you are in possession of a magician's power when editing is not only dangerous when faced with poor material, it is even more dangerous when the footage is fine. Interfering with the innate rhythm and pace of performance, for example, is especially dangerous. So, for those looking to editing as a possible career, do not contemplate it if you wish to impose yourself on others! Satisfying your psychological needs by ruining the delicate balance achieved by, amongst others, the writer, director, cameraman, designer and performers is not going to make you a major contributor to the future of cinema. A cutter is not an originator, although the effect of his work can be cathartic; he does not provide the thesis for film, but the synthesis he produces is crucial; he is seldom in at the conception, but he presides over the confinement and the birth. More often than not it is he who must re-motivate the director for whom the shooting has been less than ideal. It is a job for which there is no close analogy, but it has the satisfactions inherent in creative collaboration and, like all worthwhile occupations, it rewards in direct proportion to the degree to which you refuse to abuse the power it gives you.

A final warning: if editing gets in your blood it will stay there. There is no cure except more of it. It is truly addictive but, treated with respect, a healthy addiction that will never cease to provide the kind of satisfactions only available to those involved in a few such privileged activities.

Appendix: additional and contractual obligations of the editor

When the editing of a film is completed there are several essential tasks which mostly involve the preparation of paper work, usually for and in conjunction with the production office. In the case of a feature film there will probably exist a production and distribution agreement which lists all the delivery requirements, and the editing department should ensure that these are complied with.

FOREIGN VERSIONS

There are two specific requirements:

1   *Release script*
    If the film is to be sub-titled or dubbed into a foreign language the distributor will require release scripts. This is the dialogue and cutting continuity of the picture as edited. The release script is usually produced from the cutting copy by someone who specializes in this work or by the production secretary.

2   *Music and effects track*
    Although it is common practice to produce an M and E track if it is required specifically for foreign versions, the editor must ensure that all non-dialogue sound has been included, since some effects may have remained on the dialogue tracks during laying.

CREDITS AND TITLES

When ordering and checking titles it is important to know if there are contractual obligations with regard to size, order and length of time on the screen.

CENSOR (UK)

If the film is for theatrical release a viewing of the film will be arranged for the censor in order to obtain a certificate. On occasion the censor may call for cuts or alterations, or the producer may even decide to delete sections to comply with the censor's demands in relation to the granting of a less limiting category of certificate. This screening should therefore take place before the first answer print is made.

MUSIC CUE SHEET

A list must be prepared which shows details of all the music on the final sound track of the film, whether or not the music has been especially composed and recorded for the film. The music cue sheet is sent by the production office to the Mechanical Copyright Protection Society and to the Performing Rights Society, both of which bodies collect royalties for the copyright owners of the music.

It is important to realize that the question of music copyright is extremely complicated and it is foolhardy to incorporate *any* music into a film without obtaining clearance and indeed an understanding of the full implications of the use of music. Failure to confirm clearance and details of royalties can result in the possibility of incurring enormous expense unless the film is re-dubbed without the music, and exhibition of the film without the necessary music clearances can lead to litigation for infringement of copyright.

LIBRARY RETURNS

All sound effects or film from libraries used in the film *must* be reported to the source in order that royalties can be assessed and charged and any clearances obtained.

N.B.   Where a film is destined for theatrical release there may be other requirements specified by the country where it is produced or where it is planned to release the film. An example is the 'Form C' in Britain which is obligatory for all cinema films that are to be registered as British.

Glossary

A AND B CUTTING: The practice of conforming original material (either reversal master or negative) on two separate rolls so that optical effects can be made by double printing. Thus dissolves are assembled to include the overlaps of the two shots to allow cross-fading during printing. Not to be confused with CHEQUERBOARD cutting.

A AND B WIND: The alternative modes of winding film that has single perforations. Important when related to duping material from different sources and for indicating the form required when ordering optical sound transfers.

ACADEMY STANDARDS: Standards established by the American Academy of Motion Picture Arts and Sciences and recognized by manufacturers of equipment and film stock, e.g., the gap or pitch between perforations on stock and the corresponding alignment of sprocket wheels in editing machinery and projectors is standardized, as is the relationship between camera and projector apertures.

ACETATE: The base material used to 'carry' film emulsion. Its value lies in being 'slow burning' which makes it much safer than the old nitrate base.

ACTION: 1 The picture material as opposed to the separate sound track used in cutting.
2 The word used by the director to cue the start of a take.
3 The activity being filmed.

ACTION CUTTING (or cutting on action): The practice of using movement as the bridging mechanism at a cut, to allow a smooth change of angle and/or size of the subject in the shot. Also used to convey continuity of movement when the subject enters and exits the frame. This technique is only valid where the motivation for the cut is seen to coincide with such movement.

AMBIENT SOUND: The general background sound to any shooting situation, without which the dialogue or other specific sound seems to exist in a vacuum. Effective sound recording takes this into account and may require the use of a separate microphone to convey a sense of the 'space' in which the scene is occurring. In tracklaying separate background tracks may be required to compensate for a sync recording that has used only close perspective directional microphones.

AMERICAN CUT (or concertina cut): The practice of cutting together two shots of different size on the same camera axis.

ANSWER PRINT (or trial print): The print that represents the first attempt to grade (or 'time') the cut film correctly. The laboratory may make several tries at this before submitting such an 'answer' for approval. Its function is to allow for discussion of detailed corrections of colour balance, density and matching for the making of the show or release prints. It is also an essential stage before the making of a master dupe positive or colour reversal intermediate when a considerable number of copies are known to be required.

ASPECT RATIO (or frame format): The dimensions of the film frame in a ratio of height to width. In 16 mm 1:1·33 is normal. Wide-screen formats are 1:1·66 or 1:1·85, and, by squeezing the image, anamorphic processes provide ratios that include 1:2, 1:2·2 and 1:2·35. It is imperative that cutting takes place under conditions that imitate the intended ratio, otherwise pacing of action in and out of frame and the elimination of unwanted areas can provide problems, especially where the picture has been shot without a mask in the camera, giving excess image which will not be seen in the final print.

ASSEMBLY: The first stage in cutting after synchronizing the rushes. Usually taken to mean the joining together of chosen takes in script order, or in documentary the usable material, in shooting or chronological order.

ASYNCHRONOUS SOUND: All sound which is relevant to the circumstances of a shot but which is not synchronized to the action.

ATMOSPHERE: Usually applied to the sound that is appropriate to the background of a scene. The more general it is the less use it has. 'Atmos' should be specially recorded as a wild track to enable precise use in tracklaying. When an atmosphere contains specific references to the picture it is bad practice to rely on library recordings to substitute for the real thing. Water sounds, for instance, have an infinite variation which relate to distance, intensity and quality.

BACK PROJECTION (or rear projection): The technique of using pre-photographed images as background to the action. Preparation of such material may involve the editor. The print to be used for such projection must be obtained on double-perforation stock with negative perforations to ensure steadiness.

BACKGROUND ACTION: The action in a shot that is not intended to be the focus of attention but that requires careful matching if it is relevant to intercut material.

BACKGROUND MUSIC: This can be the bane of an editor's life. Where a scene is shot that includes music being performed or reproduced in the background the intercutting of the relevant action may be inhibited by the effect on such music. In fiction films it is often the practice to shoot scenes with a source of music visible but not actually playing and adding the music in the final mixing of the film.

BIG CLOSE-UP (B.C.U.): A shot of less than the complete head of the subject or a detail of an object.

BLEED, BLEEDING: Fuzziness around the edges of an element in the film image. A term most frequently applied to unclear superimposed titles and matted shots.

BLIMP: The sound-proof cover on a camera which prevents the noise of the camera mechanism being audible on the recorded sync sound track. Modern cameras are mostly self-blimped although this does not necessarily make them sound-proof if the camera is excessively noisy or the acoustics for the recording are bad.

BLOOP, BLOOPING: The technique of covering or removing a V-shaped section of the sound-track area to avoid a bump or click, especially at joins. This can be done by applying an opaque piece of paper or inking across the relevant section of optical track. With magnetic track it is usually achieved either by cutting out a V-section or by removing the oxide with acid. Whichever method is used, extreme care is required to avoid either damaging the track or obliterating wanted sound.

BLOW-UP: Converting 16 mm to 35 mm by laboratory process (can be applied to a similar process with 8 mm). The term is also used where the frame is optically enlarged so that the image is made to correspond to a closer shot. This is sometimes done where it is realized that the original shot is too inclusive. The resultant degradation in quality may not be worth the cost.

BRIDGING SHOT: The kind of shot that allows a smoother or more acceptable transition than a direct cut. Sometimes useful in pacing the junction between sequences but it can be an excuse for a badly conceived structure.

BUILD-UP: Dramatic cutting leading to a climax in the action. The term is also used colloquially in the cutting room for the insertion of frames to designate a missing section or shot in the cutting copy or work print.

BUTT SPLICE: A join between two pieces of film without an overlap – facilitated by the application of tape across the end frame of each section.

BUZZ TRACK: Sound that represents the 'presence' in a room or space in which a recording usually of a voice or voices has been made. Most commonly obtained to allow insertion or bridging when laying up dialogue or narration.

CAMERA SHEET (or negative report): The information on a standard form that describes the precise technical details of shooting for laboratory reference, including film emulsion, day or night, good and bad takes, footages etc.

CAPTION: Title, descriptive text or translation placed between shots or superimposed on them.

CELL-SIDE: The opposite side to the emulsion on a piece of film, usually recognizable because it is shiny and reflective.

CEMENT JOINER (or cement splicer): Allows for joining of pieces of film by overlapping, and the application of a form of glue or cement. Now superseded in cutting rooms but still predominant in negative and original cutting. Also used for repairs by projectionists since it gives a longer lasting and more reliable join. It involves the removal of frames from the shots to be joined.

CENTRE TRACK: The standard position of the audio signal on magnetic film. See EDGE TRACK.

CHANGE-OVER: The co-ordination of the start of a new reel of film with the end of the previous one during projection (facilitated by reference to CUE DOTS), so that the film appears to run continuously.

CHEAT: The repositioning of a character or object in a way convenient for taking a shot that is not consistent with the positioning in other shots. Allows for reverse angles and better visibility of facial expressions, etc. It may be made necessary by shooting in restricted space and/or the limits presented by the angle of view of the lens.

CHEQUERBOARD: Method of conforming original or negative to cutting copy or work print whereby *every* shot is put on to alternate rolls with spacing in the other roll. Primarily used to eliminate splices in printing. Also allows for fades and dissolves during printing. See A AND B CUTTING.

CINCHING, CINCH MARKS: The result of a roll of film being pulled tight on a core or spool. The friction in the roll causes scratches where dust or abrasive particles are present.

CINEMA-VÉRITÉ (or Ciné-Vérité): A style of film-making begun in

Europe in the 1950s, in which the use of light-weight cameras and recorders encouraged a direct approach to the capturing of 'reality'. Now taken to mean an unstructured approach to the filming of documentary material with little or no attempt to influence the events being filmed.

CINEX-STRIP (or Cinex): The printing of a few frames of each shot in a camera roll as reference for grading or timing the material, thus determining the optimum printer light.

CIRCLED TAKES: The practice of circling the preferred takes listed on the CAMERA SHEET, to indicate to the laboratory which ones should be printed.

CLAPPERBOARD (or slate): The device to aid synchronization, filmed at the beginning or end of each take. The 'clapping' of the hinged section provides an exact visual and aural reference point. It also gives slate and take numbers.

CLICK TRACK: A substitute for a metronome in the form of a sound track with regular clicks inserted, enabling the conductor to retain the correct tempo in recording music to the cut film.

CLOSE-UP (C.U.): Taken to mean the complete head of a person. M.C.U., B.C.U. and E.C.U. are tighter versions of the basic C.U. shot. With a small object a C.U. would mean that the object fills the frame. Applied to a large object it can refer to the most significant detail filling that frame.

CODE NUMBERS (edge numbers or rubber numbers): A method of numbering film and/or magnetic stock to provide a reference for logging purposes and corresponding sync. Usually consists of 6 or 8 letters and numbers which progress at 1-foot intervals by a digit at a time. On 16mm, coding machines can give numbering at 6-inch intervals.

COLOUR CORRECTION: The process by which film is adjusted for correct colour balance in the printing. It must be specifically requested when sending exposed material to the laboratories since colour rush prints are normally supplied at a mean printer light without attempts being made to rectify variations in exposure and colour values.

C.R.I. (Colour Reversal Intermediate): This is made when a dupe is required either for optical work or protection of master material. It eliminates the need for the interpositive/internegative process although this may still be the preferred method.

COMBINED PRINT (composite print or married print): A print that combines the matching picture and sound of a completed film.

COMPILATION FILM: A film edited from material gathered from a number of sources on the same subject, possibly including specially shot film but also consisting of library footage and material duplicated from other films. The coherence of such films usually depends upon a linking narration or voice-over. Prime examples are documentaries on war and obituaries.

COMPLEMENTARY ANGLES: Shots that are matched between two or more subjects in the same scene and are calculated to cut together.

COMPOSITE PRINT *see* COMBINED PRINT

CONCERTINA CUT *see* AMERICAN CUT

CONFORMING: Process of cutting master or original negative to match the cutting copy or work print in preparation for printing.

CONTACT-PRINTER: Machine for printing material where the negative or original is kept in contact with the raw stock. 'Continuous contact-printers' are used for printing rushes at high speed.

CONTINUITY: Usually describes the effort to maintain consistency in the details of the staging of scenes for the camera. This includes continuity of movement and of the relationship between action and dialogue, and details of dress and any placing or use of objects. The continuity person is charged specifically with scrupulously observing such detail, pointing out any deficiency and recording the details of each take, including deviations, in the continuity notes. A really observant continuity person will also pick up problems of matching between shots (angles, eyelines, etc.) and even problematical variations in lighting. The value of this function in the filming of drama cannot be overestimated.

CONTINUITY CUTTING: The editing of sequences so that the action and progression of the scene matches the natural flow captured in the various shots, thus avoiding a disjointed effect. Where a scene is shot in a variety of set-ups this may entail judicious shortening of dialogue and/or action whilst maintaining the desired smoothness and plausibility.

CONTRAST: Photographically, contrast is the ratio between the most dense and least dense areas expressed in terms of GAMMA. Contrast can vary between 'flat' where there is little range of tones, to HIGH CONTRAST ('contrasty') where there is only very slight gradation between the lightest and darkest areas of the image. Printing can vary the contrast range, but only within the limits established by the original material.

CORE (or bobbin): A plastic centre on which film is wound. In most cases the core has an indentation for engaging with the 'tooth' on the take-up mechanism and is designated as female. Exceptionally, 'male' cores may be necessary where the mechanism being used incorporates the indentation or slot.

COVER: The collection of shots taken for each particular sequence. Conventional cover includes everything from wide shots to matching close-ups.

CRAB SHOT: A shot that covers lateral movement from the side. The camera faces the action but moves in a crab-like fashion.

CRANE SHOT: Literally a shot that incorporates a vertical movement obtained by mounting the camera on a crane. This facilitates elevation from ground level to a height above the action.

CREDITS: The titles on a film which 'credit' crew and cast involved in the production.

CROSSCUT: The method of INTERCUTTING the primary elements in dramatic sequences, especially where the action is leading to a dramatic climax, e.g. crosscutting between the participants in a gun fight.

CUE: Each section that is broken out of the cutting copy for post-sychronization. In the notes that are prepared each cue will have a number corresponding to that marked on the film.

CUE DOTS: The marks, usually appearing in the top right-hand corner of the frame, that allow the projectionist to change over between reels. A cue-dot marker normally removes a circular area of the emulsion over four frames. These cue dots are placed at two set points towards the end of a reel, to allow for both starting the projector and changing over the lamp. The standard position is for the first set of dots to start at 192 frames from the end of the reel and for the second set to start at 24 frames.

CUE LINE: The line that is drawn on the cutting copy to provide a visual cue for post-synchronization.

CUE SHEET: The various forms of detailed and enumerated information sheets, used as reference for different stages in the post-production sound-recording processes. Thus cue sheets are used for post-sync, music recording and for the final mixing of the film.

CUTAWAY: The much maligned – perhaps justifiably – kind of shot which, as its name implies, shows a person or object that requires cutting away from the dominant focus of a scene. It is used to bridge shots that do not cut together and to allow for editing/shortening of the action in a continuous shot. A form of 'cheating' that some film-makers consider dishonest.

CUTTING COPY: The WORK PRINT of a film or, more specifically, the progressively evolving structured visuals of a film.

CUTTING ON ACTION see ACTION CUTTING

DAILIES see RUSHES

DAY FOR NIGHT (D/N): The shooting of scenes which, by control of exposure, use of filters and specified processing requirements, gives the effect of night despite being shot during daylight. The editor must be aware of such material both in assessing the rushes and in controlling any subsequent printing.

DEFINITION: The quality of an image as it is affected by variations in focus, exposure and lighting. The term is also used in relation to the clarity of sound. The definition of picture and sound can also be affected by the circumstances of projection or reproduction.

DEGAUSSER: A device which erases recordings or demagnetizes tape, film or sound heads. Also used on tape joiners which have become magnetized.

DENSITY: The variable degree of light-stopping power in a photographic image.

DESATURATION: The reduction of the degree of colour in a film image resulting eventually in a monochromatic effect.

DEVELOP: The process which renders the latent image on film into a permanent image by use of a chemical reaction.

DIAGONAL CUT: The method used on magnetic film to reduce the noise at a splice, facilitated by a guillotine on the splicer which is set at an oblique angle to the frame.

DIALOGUE: Speech that is obviously or apparently emanating from the person or persons visible in the scene. It is either seen in sync or heard over other characters involved in the scene.

DIRECT CINEMA: The type of film that depends on pictures and sound indigenous to the situations being filmed. The film 'speaks for itself' without the superimposing, by voice-over or other means, of the attitude of the film-maker. Direct Cinema also puts severe limitations on the way the material can be manipulated in the cutting room. It implies a more disciplined approach than its immediate precursor CINEMA-VÉRITÉ.

DISCONTINUITY: A fault in the CONTINUITY during the filming of a scene.

DISSOLVE (or mix): The effect produced by the fading out at the end of a shot overlapping with the fading in of the next (see FADES). Can be produced in the camera but now almost exclusively created by optical dupe or in A and B printing. Originally used to mean change of time and/or place, but it has developed into a general facet of film language that complements the pacing or mood of a film. Dissolves can vary in length from less than a second upwards. However, A and B dissolves can only be obtained at specific lengths usually ranging from 8 to 96 frames ($\frac{1}{3}$ second to 4 seconds).

DOLLY: A platform with wheels on which the camera is mounted to allow smooth movement.

DOUBLE-HEAD PROJECTION: Running the film in the cutting room or on a projector with the sound track separate from the picture.

DROP-SHADOW: Used in titling to improve definition of lettering especially when titles are superimposed over live action backgrounds. Provides a darker area below and to the side of the titles.

DUB: The process of re-recording sound, specifically to replace dialogue or effects. The term is a source of some confusion, since in England dubbing is coterminous with mixing (see MIX), while in the USA it refers only to post-synchronization (particularly in the making of foreign language versions).

DUBBING CUE SHEET: The written information that acts as a guide for the sound mixer. It is known in the USA as the mixing cue sheet because of the variations in terminology referred to above.

DUBBING SESSION: Specifically a dialogue-replacement recording session in the USA. The term is used more generally in England to describe the processes involved in mixing the sound on a film.

DUPE, DUPING: To make or the making of duplicate material from an existing negative, print or reversal master.

DYE-TRANSFER: A system of printing that involves the production of three colour separation positives (yellow, cyan and magenta). These dyed images or matrices are then transferred to blank film and allow for the printing of large numbers of release prints without further use of the original negative. This is a Technicolor process which has now unfortunately been discontinued.

ECHO CHAMBER/PLATE: A source of reverberation attached to a sound-recording studio, connected to the mixing desk to facilitate instant and variable use when required.

EDGE NUMBERS see CODE NUMBERS, KEY NUMBERS

EDGE STRIPE: A magnetic stripe used to carry sound as an alternative to optical sound, usually in COMBINED PRINTS.

EDGE TRACK: The standard position in the USA for the magnetic sound. See CENTRE TRACK.

EDITING BENCH (or sync bench): The table that normally carries the synchronizer and rewinds when such are incorporated in the cutting process.

EFFECTS (F.X.) see SOUND EFFECTS

EMULSION: The coating that is carried by the film base. In its unexposed form it is light-sensitive and has chemical properties which allow the development of the latent image during processing. In its printed form, the emulsion gives form to the photographed image both in terms of density and variations in colour.

EMULSION POSITION: This refers to the geometry of the film image. The image is correctly viewed either through the base or with the emulsion to the eye.

EQUALIZATION: The alteration of sound frequencies to achieve a better balance, or even to remove unwanted signals from existing recordings. It is especially valuable in improving the clarity of voice tracks.

ESTABLISHING SHOT: The wide shot of a location or set that presents the full context of a scene to the viewer, thus allowing subsequent fragments of the scene to be perceived within this totality. In editing it is often more effective to refrain from showing this until it is dramatically relevant.

E.C.U.: Extreme close-up.

E.L.S.: Extreme long shot.

EXPOSITION: The early scenes in a film which lay the foundations of situation and characters in the plot.

FADES: Visual or aural gradual revelation or obliteration of the image or sound: thus fade in and fade out. These effects are often used coterminously on both picture and sound but should also be considered useful when treated separately. Most conventionally, fades indicate the beginning and end of scenes.

FILTER: Devices used in shooting, usually in front of the camera lens, to accentuate or reduce specific aspects of the image to be photographed, e.g. colour and density. Also the device which alters the reproduction of selected frequencies in sound recording.

FINAL MIX: The combination of various sound tracks into one composite master, often after the intermediate stage of pre-mixing.

FINE CUT: The later stages of picture editing (after the ROUGH CUT) when only minor adjustments are being contemplated before the final cut is agreed upon.

FINE GRAIN: The term is applied to emulsion that provides a high definition and resolution of the image by incorporating extra-fine particles of silver. It is consequently used in making master duplicate material especially for optical work. More appropriately applied to black-and-white film.

FLASHBACK: Shots or sequences that convey events or information which precede the time established as the present in a film.

FLOP-OVER: Reversing the image laterally. It can be valuable for restoring 'eyelines' or continuity of movement to the correct left-to-right appearance. Achieved by optical process in the laboratory.

FOCUS: The definition of an image, both as photographed and in projection. Loss of focus or differential focus in the image can have a crucial effect on the usability of material when editing.

FOOTAGE: The accumulated material for a film. Also the measurement of film and the precise reading at a given point in a reel indicated on a FOOTAGE COUNTER.

FOOTAGE COUNTER: A mechanical or electronic device that indicates the progressive number of feet in a reel of film being run on an editing device or projector.

FRAME FORMAT see ASPECT RATIO

FREEZE-FRAME: The repeated printing of a single frame for a predetermined number of times, thus 'freezing' the action. Can be used in conjunction with or separate from part of the action before or after the particular frame by including part of the original shot in the dupe.

FRONT PROJECTION: Inclusion of separate material as background to the action of a scene by projecting it from in front of the scene being filmed. Usually incorporates a special screen behind the action and supplementary lighting on the foreground subjects.

GAMMA: A way of measuring photographic contrast. It equals the density increase in an image divided by the log of the exposure increase over a specified range.

GATE: Generally the section in a camera or projector mechanism where the film passes behind the lens. More exactly the hinged section that carries the pressure plate.

GAUGE: A convenient reference to film size by measurement of its width. Thus 8 mm, 16 mm, 35 mm and 70 mm.

GRADATION: The variation in tonal values in a photographic image.

GRADING (or timing): The work done by the grader or (in the USA) timer in selecting the colour balance and intensity and the overall density to be applied to film when preparing for printing. In practice the grader aims at a programme of values which are automatically cued in the consecutive exposure of scenes on the printer.

GRAININESS, GRAINY: The apparently distinguishable particles in an image where poor RESOLUTION has caused the silver particles to group together in a way that provides an unsatisfactory rendition of the original scene. It can be caused by sub-standard lenses, slow stock or inadequate exposure or lighting.

HEAD: The start or front of a roll of film. Also the device which enables sound to be picked up from a track passing in front of or over it.

HEADPHONES (or head-set): Small sound receivers which fit over the head and are adjustable to the position of the ears of the user. Used by recordists as a monitoring device and also valuable for artists and conductors when recording post-sync and music.

HIGH CONTRAST: Applied to photographic images that do not exhibit a gradual range from dark to light. Also applied to stock that is designed specifically to exhibit this lack of gradation. Especially suited to the shooting of titles and optical sound.

HIGH KEY: Images that exhibit a tendency to lighter tones. Also lighting that is calculated to achieve such an effect.

HOLD: Takes that may be printed later but are not required for immediate use. Also the static section at the beginning and end of camera movement which is invaluable in cutting.

HORSE: The device on an EDITING BENCH that is designed for mounting rolls of film by the insertion of rods through apertures in vertical sections. Especially valuable when working with many short sections of film.

HOT SPLICER (or heat splicer): A joiner that incorporates a heating device in the elements. These are clamped together to increase the efficiency of the cement that is bonding the two sections of film.

IN SYNC: The state of picture and sound material when they are in correct relationship to each other with regard to synchronization.

IN THE CAN: A colloquial expression to describe completion of shooting either of a shot, a sequence or the whole film.

INCHING: The process of moving the film frame by frame through a transport mechanism for close examination.

INCOMING SHOT: The shot *after* any cut as opposed to the previous or outgoing shot.

INSERT: A shot that is designed to be cut into the body of another shot or sequence that focuses attention on a particular aspect or detail of the scene.

INTERCUT: Editing by juxtaposition of elements that are related by time, place or action or where the establishment of such a relationship *depends on* such juxtaposition.

INTERMEDIATE: A process in the laboratory that is necessary or valuable in proceeding from the original form of the material to some required duplicate – thus 'internegative' and 'interpositive'.

INTERMITTENT MOVEMENT: The frame-by-frame movement in a camera, projector or printer that allows the recording or reproduction of images which, when combined, give the illusion of continuous movement when such movement proceeds above the speed at which the eye can perceive the individual static frames.

IRIS: An adjustable device that controls the amount of light passing through a lens. Also the effect gained by obscuring the outer area of the frame both in the camera or in printing. Used as a substitute for fades although this practice was more common in the silent era.

JACK: A convenient plug device for connecting into sockets during sound recording and reproduction.

JOIN: The splicing of two sections of film at a cut.

JOINER see CEMENT JOINER; TAPE JOINER

JUMP CUT: Strictly speaking the effect obtained by removing a section from the middle of a shot and joining the remaining head and tail of the shot, thus provoking a jump in the action. Loosely applied to any such abrupt change that implies a missing part of the original visual continuity.

KEY NUMBERS (or edge numbers): Numbers that are exposed on to film stock at regular intervals, and that progress by one digit each time. Printed on to copies they provide a co-ordinating reference for matching. On 16mm they usually occur each 6 inches or 20 frames and, on 35mm, every foot or 16 frames. When checking work or rush prints, it is important to ensure that these numbers have been duplicated. Where no code numbers have been applied, key numbers can provide an alternative for logging.

KULESHOV EFFECT: Named after experiments conducted by Lev Kuleshov in Russia in the 1920s. In general this term describes the effects obtained through juxtaposition in editing – most notably Kuleshov proved that the interpretation of human facial expressions can be changed by altering the shots with which they are intercut. So he showed that 'meaning' is not dependent on a shot alone but also on the shot or shots placed around it.

LATENT IMAGE: The image formed on photographic emulsion by exposure to light. It is made visible by developing the film.

LAYING TRACKS see TRACKLAYING

LEADER: Extra film placed at the front or end of material which acts as protection to the body of the film and also functions as identification and for threading through editing machines and projectors. It can be spacer marked up with sync reference and details of the contents of the roll or it can be a standard leader with count-down markings, etc. Sync leaders should be of a specified length for projection purposes (see PROJECTION LEADER).

LEVEL SYNC: The relationship between separate picture and sound material that is sync-marked in parallel. Necessary for distinguishing from PRINTING SYNC where the sound has to be advanced by a specific number of frames for composite or married printing.

LIBRARY SHOTS: Visuals available from stock footage for duplication and insertion into the body of specially shot material. Thus the Eiffel Tower to establish Paris where the scene is a studio set – although much more subtle use can be made of good library material.

LIBRARY SOUND: Stock music and effects available for use on films either from tape or disc. These can be transferred to film for tracklaying or played in from source during mixing.

LIP SYNC: Speech that is coincidental with the image of the speaker.

LIQUID GATE: A printer gate that immerses the film in liquid. It eliminates scratches by filling them in and prevents refractions during exposure. Not to be confused with WET GATE.

LIVE ACTION: Applied to the shooting of living things as opposed to abstract or animation filming.

LOG (or LOG SHEET): The written catalogue of film material, usually cross-referencing KEY or CODE NUMBERS with SLATE and TAKE numbers, with additional shorthand notes of the nature of each shot.

L.S.: Long shot.

LOOPS, LOOPING: In editing, loops are made of sections of film and/or sound for two purposes. Firstly, for post-synchronization of dialogue or effects and, secondly, for use as continuous background effects during mixing to avoid laying up a long continuous length. The loop is joined head to tail for continuous running on projectors or sound reproducers. The length of loops must be carefully determined to allow for easy running and convenient use.

LOW ANGLE: A shot taken from below the subject, i.e. any shot of a human being which is markedly below eye level. Usually chosen for dramatic emphasis.

LOW KEY: Lighting to produce an image that is dominated by darker tones, or picture that demonstrates this quality.

MAGNETIC HEAD: A sound component that acts in contact with magnetic film or tape to record, reproduce or erase sound.

MAGNETIC MASTER: The sound track that carries the final mixed sound to be used for transfer to the optical or MAGNETIC STRIPE which is combined with the picture for show or release copies. Also used for DOUBLE-HEAD PROJECTION, although it is safer to run a copy.

MAGNETIC SOUND FILM: Film that uses iron oxide as the coating on which sound is recorded and reproduced. See OPTICAL SOUND.

MAGNETIC STRIPE: The strip of iron oxide placed on film in the normal sound-track position, usually as an alternative to OPTICAL SOUND for release prints.

MAGNETIC TAPE: $\frac{1}{4}$-in. sound tape.

MAGNETIC TRACK: Usually applied to magnetic sound film carrying various kinds of sound for use in the cutting process or laid up for mixing. (Note: the word magnetic in all its uses is commonly abbreviated to mag.)

MARRIED PRINT see COMBINED PRINT

MASK: A device used mostly in cameras and printers to limit the area of the frame that is exposed to light. Thus a mask can alter the ASPECT RATIO and it can facilitate split-screen filming by alternately covering matching parts of the frame.

MASTER: Applies to both picture and sound. With picture it can refer to the printed camera original from reversal film and also to a timed, graded or corrected print (master positive) from which duplicates can be made. In sound, master refers to the final mixed track or the original recording or tape or sound film of any important component, e.g. music master or sync master.

MASTER SHOT: The shot that covers a whole scene both in terms of duration and in containing all relevant action. It is conventionally shot first so that all COVER can be subsequently filmed to match.

MATCH(ING) ACTION: Cutting that uses the process of any movement as a device for providing a smooth transition between cuts. Although cutting on action is a useful technique it is not a substitute for proper analysis of the motivation for a cut.

MATRIX see DYE-TRANSFER

MATTE: A device for limiting the area of the frame to be exposed either on the camera or on a separate strip of film in the printer. In the latter case the shape and position of the matte can be altered frame by frame to match the area to be 'matted' – it is thus called 'travelling matte'.

M.C.U.: Medium close-up shot.

M.L.S.: Medium long shot.

M.S.: Medium shot.

MISE-EN-SCENE (or staging): The manipulation of all the elements which contribute to the filming of a scene. Primarily the setting, props, costumes, lighting and action and the way they relate to the camera. Proper consideration of mise-en-scene includes an awareness of the contribution envisaged in the editing.

MIX: Applied to sound, this describes the process of combining two or more sound sources into a single recording. As a noun it refers to the resultant sound track. With regard to picture, see DISSOLVE.

MIXER: The person who performs or co-ordinates the process of mixing.

MODULATION: Variations in a sound signal, either as heard or as it exists in a recording.

MONTAGE: The term was originally used to describe creative editing by the Russians in the 1920s; it was then applied to quick cutting often with the use of opticals exhibited in Hollywood films of the 1930s, usually for sequences that provided shorthand descriptions of events or narrative progression. The French use the term to describe editing per se. Nowadays montage is most usually taken to mean any cutting that assembles a number of shots in an impressionistic fashion so as to achieve an overall effect not inherent in the separate elements. It is often backed by a dense sound track which normally includes music.

MOOD MUSIC: Music used to complement or support the atmosphere and emotional content of a scene.

M.O.S.: An American term applied to shots made without sound. It is said to be derived from a Germanic/English rendering of 'without sound' as 'mit-out sound'. Elsewhere such shots are described as MUTE.

M AND E TRACK: Music and effects track. Usually arrived at in pre-mixing or, in any case, as a separate part of the mixing process. Invaluable for alternative versions of a final sound track as it allows for foreign dialogue to be used to replace the original version without recourse to all the original tracks. It also simplifies the balancing of the voice tracks against the other sound.

MUTE: Shots without sound. See M.O.S.

NARRATION (commentary or voice-over): Words spoken over the film either by an anonymous person or by a person or actor who figures in the film. Can be first person or third person in style. The words are not related to the synchronous dialogue.

NEGATIVE CUTTING: Conforming the camera negative to the cutting copy or work print in preparation for printing.

NEGATIVE REPORT *see* CAMERA SHEET

N.G. TAKES: Takes that are no good and therefore not worth using in the cutting. In practice N.G. takes may be developed with the rest of the material but not printed.

NODDY: A colloquial term describing a shot of an interviewer nodding, obtained for use as a CUTAWAY during editing.

OBLIGATORY SCENE: The scene in most narrative films without which the crux of the dramatic action is not established. It is conventionally placed between exposition and the development of the specific focus of the plot. In scripting shooting and cutting it therefore requires particular care and attention.

OFF-CAMERA: Beyond the margins of the frame.

OFF-LAYING: The process of splitting sound tracks, especially dialogue, to allow for balancing and equalization during the mix.

OFF-MIKE: Sound that is not picked up by the microphone at a usable level, e.g. feed lines from a character out of shot. Such dialogue must be replaced if it exists within the body of a shot as cut. It is usually available from the track of a complementary shot.

OFF-SCALE: Beyond the limits of the series of printer lights. Applied to material that is either so under- or over-exposed that a usable rendition of the scene is impossible.

OFF-SCREEN (O.S.): Action not seen by the camera but often pertinent. Sometimes conveyed by sound such as voice or effects.

O.K. TAKES: Designation on CAMERA SHEETS and continuity sheets of shots which are good enough to be printed. Does not necessarily imply satisfaction with performance, but is an indication that both the cameraman and the sound recordist are satisfied.

ONE-LIGHT PRINT: A print in which all the scenes in a roll are made at the same printer light setting. The setting is determined by analysing the range of exposure and striking an average which will provide a reasonable print of all the shots, assuming the range is not too extreme.

OPTICAL EFFECTS (or opticals): The penumbra of effects obtainable by use of the optical printer at the laboratory. Includes DISSOLVES, FADES and WIPES.

OPTICAL PRINT: The print that is produced by involving the process available through an optical printer.

OPTICAL PRINTER: The device that, by projecting the original images and re-photographing them, can facilitate various alterations in the nature of those images, including enlargement, reduction, speeding up, slowing down, freezing and many special effects.

OPTICAL SOUND: A photographic means of recording and reproducing sound. Now almost exclusively of the variable area variety, although previously also available in a variable density form. Optical sound is still the predominant system for RELEASE PRINTING but has been superseded by MAGNETIC SOUND for shooting and cutting purposes.

ORIGINAL: Specifically the material on which the images have been photographed (also applied similarly to sound), i.e. original negative and reversal original.

ORTHOCHROMATIC FILM (ORTHO): Black-and-white film that is not red-sensitive, i.e. does not reproduce the red part of the spectrum properly.

OUT OF SYNC: Any situation where the picture and sound track are misaligned when it is intended that they should be IN SYNC.

OUTGOING SHOT: The shot before a cut as opposed to the next or INCOMING SHOT.

OUT-TAKES (or outs): Those takes that are not selected for use either after shooting or when cutting. Not to be confused with SPARES.

OVERLAP: The shooting of part of a scene so that it occurs in two or more shots to provide choice in cutting points. Also the carrying of sound from one shot over the beginning or end of the one adjacent to it.

OVERLAPPING DIALOGUE: The overlap of the speech of one character with that of another. This can be a nuisance if it occurs in the shooting at a point that is valuable for cutting but, on the other hand, it can be manufactured in cutting to provide the sense of interruption or to increase the pace of a scene.

OVER-THE-SHOULDER SHOT (O.S.S.): Any shot framed with a character's shoulder and/or part of his head on one side of the frame, with his back to the camera, usually looking at another character.

PAN: A shot that moves laterally from a static camera position (as opposed to TRACKING). Can involve following the movement of the action in the shot. Also used for movement between two characters not contained within the camera frame. If there is variation from the original vertical point of view of the shot it is described as pan-and-tilt.

PANCHROMATIC FILM: Black-and-white film that is sensitive to the whole spectrum.

PARALLEL ACTION: The shooting and cutting of two or more sequences of events so as to convey the impression of their occurring at the same time. Usually – although not necessarily – reaching a conclusion by the two sequences merging into the same space. Most effective when it is implied that there is a positive connection between the separate events. Edwin S. Porter's *The Great Train Robbery* (1903) is usually cited as the first sophisticated use of this technique.

PERSISTENCE OF VISION: The phenomenon without which the 'moving picture' could not exist: the retention of an image by the eye beyond the time at which it is 'visible'. The eye does not register a flicker between the static frames of film so long as the separate images are photographed and shown at a speed above 16 frames per second assuming the normal viewing conditions for film.

PICK-UP SHOT: An additional shot taken of a section in a scene which it is felt has been inadequately covered by the other shots. It is taken either at the end of the shooting for a particular scene or after the material has been processed and viewed.

PLAYBACK: The playing of previously recorded sound, both for reference or simply to check its quality.

PLAYBACK TRACK: A sound track specifically recorded for playing back during the shooting of the relevant scene. Most commonly vocal music for singers to mime to, although also used extensively for instrumental and dance sequences.

P.O.V. (point of view): Shots taken from the established view of a person or persons in a scene, usually to be intercut with shots of that person or persons watching the scene shown in the P.O.V.

POST-SYNCHRONIZATION: The process of replacing dialogue and/or effects by re-recording with reference to the original picture and (if available) the sync sound. Requires precise handling to match the appropriate visual details, especially with lip movement in dialogue. Also describes the dubbing of foreign language voices for overseas versions of a film.

PRE-MIX: To mix some elements of the sound for a film as an intermediary process towards the final mix. Where there are many tracks it is often necessary to pre-mix each element, e.g. dialogue, music and effects. The most common pre-mix, however, is of music and effects before adding the dialogue and/or narration.

PRESENCE: The background sound that conveys the sense of an identifiable space. Without room presence all other sound seems artificial.

PRINTER-LIGHT: The source of illumination in a printer. Also the range of illumination levels that allows for variation in printing to compensate for variable exposure.

PRINTING SYNC: The specific sound advance required for printing picture and sound together. For 35mm optical sound the advance is 20 frames, for 16mm optical 26 frames and for 16mm magnetic it is 28 frames. *See* LEVEL SYNC.

PRINT-THROUGH: The undesirable recording of an audio signal on to the layer of magnetic tape adjacent to the one on which it is meant to register.

PROJECTION LEADER: A section of film joined to the front of a reel with standard markings which act as reference for the projectionist in lacing up and in changing over between reels.

PROTECTION SHOT: An admission of failure or insecurity. This is a shot that provides the editor with a convenient bridging device to cover bad continuity or mismatching of angles.

QUARTER-INCH TAPE: The usual vehicle for original sound recordings when filming.

REACTION SHOT: Any shot or part of a shot that is taken or used to show the reaction of one or more characters to action and/or sound that precedes it.

REAR PROJECTION *see* BACK PROJECTION

REDUCTION PRINTING: The process of duplicating a film on to stock of a narrower gauge, e.g. 35mm reduced to 16mm.

REEL: The spool that carries film or the roll of film that is so carried.

RELEASE PRINT: Any print of a film that is made for distribution and exhibition.

RESOLUTION: The ability of a lens or emulsion to render fine detail in a photographic image.

REVERSAL FILM: Film that combines the function of negative and positive thus producing a print without an intermediary process. Thus, when reversal original is used for shooting, the same stock becomes a print after processing. In practice a reversal work print is made to protect this original master.

REVERSE ANGLE: Any shooting position or shot that is the reverse perspective to a shot already taken. In practice reverse angles are seldom at 180° to each other since film grammar demands that shots which must be intercut are framed *within* an arc of less than 180°.

REWIND: The mechanism for and the act of rewinding film.

ROLL: Any section of film that is wound on itself or on a spool or core (bobbin).

ROUGH CUT: The stage in cutting between ASSEMBLY of the rushes and a FINE CUT. Used to establish the chronology of scenes but does not involve any attempt to refine specific cuts. Only valuable if there are problems about the overall structure which need to be faced before fine cutting commences.

RUBBER NUMBERS *see* CODE NUMBERS

RUN-UP: To run a section of film prior to the shot or sequence being worked on or viewed, either over a previous sequence or a leader.

RUSHES (or dailies): The unedited picture and sound material of any shoot which are made ready for synchronization and viewing as soon as possible after shooting, and from which the film is cut.

SATURATION: The degree of colour in film material. Useful when discussing the GRADING of a particular shot, sequence or film – thus de-saturated, highly saturated.

SCENE: Each coherent but separate unit of dramatic action in the script or finished film.

SCRATCH PRINT (or slash dupe): Usually a one-light reversal print made from the cutting copy or work print for dubbing purposes.

SCREEN DIRECTION: The way movement or the positioning of subjects within the frame is controlled to make sense in terms of film grammar. Continuity of screen direction must be maintained during shooting and cutting to avoid disorientating the audience. Thus, two characters in a simple scene must retain the same relationship in all shots unless a new position is established either by camera movement or by showing the characters themselves changing their position.

SET-UP: Any particular camera position. Several shots can be taken from the same set-up, even if they are separated in terms of the script. A set-up usually implies continuity of lighting.

SHOOTING RATIO: A measure of the amount of film shot compared with the length of the finished film. Thus 5:1 indicates that five times the footage of the completed film was shot. Especially useful as a way of estimating the stock needed to shoot a film, by multiplying the timed script by the expected ratio. This budgeted ratio compared to an analysis of the actual ratio as shooting progresses is a device much used by producers and film accountants to judge the variance and to estimate overage.

SHOT LIST: A more or less elaborate listing of shots usually including slate numbers and an abbreviated description, either of the action in dramatic films or of the subject for documentary purposes.

SIBILANCE: Refers to the hiss created in speaking and recording of words that contain an emphatic 'S' sound. Can result in problems if the resulting sound is unattractive. Sometimes caused by positioning the speaker too close to the microphone.

SIGNAL-TO-NOISE RATIO: The relationship between the specific sounds required in a recording and the level of noise present in the background. Thus the lower the ratio is in decibels the more likely it is that the required sound will lack clarity.

SLASH DUPE *see* SCRATCH PRINT

SLATE: The term for, or the device and process of, denoting a shot during filming.

SLUG: A section of spacing, leader or junk film used as BUILD-UP.

S.M.P.T.E.: Society of Motion Picture and Television Engineers. A professional body in the USA that has established a number of standards and procedures with regard to film and television techniques. These have gained virtually universal acceptance.

SOFT CUT: A very short dissolve conveying the effect of a merging of two images but without implying passage of time or change of scene.

SOFT FOCUS: Either a deliberate or accidental effect where the image exhibits a slight lack of sharpness. Used deliberately especially on close-ups of female stars to enhance their appearance. As an accidental effect this can ruin a shot by spoiling a part or whole of the image.

SOUND ADVANCE: The number of frames between any picture and its appropriate sound as positioned for PRINTING SYNC.

SOUND EFFECTS: Any sound other than dialogue, narration or music that exists in or is added to the sound tracks.

SOUND HEAD: The optical or magnetic device that picks up sound during recording or playback.

SOUND LOOP: A section of sound (usually of effects) that is joined head to tail for continuous running during mixing, normally for use as additional background sound when required.

SOUND REPORT: The sound equivalent of the CAMERA SHEET, giving details of all recording and commenting on the quality of each take.

SOUND SPEED: The rate at which sound film is run through equipment – either 24 or 25 frames per second. Established at a time when it was necessary to regulate filming speed so as to provide consistency in the reproduction of sound. Such consistency was, of course, not an absolute prerequisite in the days of silent films.

SPACER: Blank leader or gash film that is used as such in building up sound tracks.

SPARES: Takes that are usable but not yet incorporated in the cutting copy. These are filed separately for easy access.

SPECIAL EFFECTS: Shots or the shooting of film that include abnormal photographic techniques. Also applied to explosions and other shooting using special devices.

SPLICE: The process of joining pieces of film together or the resultant joins.

SPLICER: Any device used for joining film. See CEMENT JOINER; TAPE JOINER.

SPOOL: A reel for holding wound-up film, either solid or of the split variety. The latter is more useful in editing since it allows for easier handling.

SPOT EFFECTS: Sound effects that require precise 'spotting' in tracklaying and mixing, e.g. gun shots, door slams and footsteps.

SQUAWK BOX: A derogatory term describing the kind of loudspeaker once prevalent in cutting rooms, referring to the poor quality of sound reproduction obtained from them. Higher fidelity equipment is now more normal.

STAGING see MISE-EN-SCENE

START-MARK: The mark on a frame that provides a reference for projection and/or synchronized running of separate picture and sound rolls.

STATIC: Marks caused by a discharge of static electricity during the photographic process. They result from friction between the stock and the machinery through which it is being run. They cannot be removed from the film and thus may cause rejection of the affected material.

STEP PRINTER/PRINTING: The machine or process that prints film by holding each frame still during exposure, thus allowing for special treatment of each individual frame.

STOCK FOOTAGE (or stock shots): Film that is held for use in films requiring material other than that specially shot. May be of an exotic or unrepeatable nature but can also be general establishing material.

STRAIGHT CUT: Used to differentiate the normal joining together of shots from those involving optical effects.

STRIPPING: The process of removing all extraneous sound from dialogue tracks to assist in the creation of clean recordings during mixing.

SUBJECTIVE CAMERA, SUBJECTIVE SHOOTING: Filming from an angle that is meant to imitate the point of view of a character in the film, or positioning the camera so as to give the audience the experience of direct involvement with the scene. The action is sometimes staged as if the camera is the focus of attention in the scene, whether or not we identify with another character's point of view.

SUB-TITLE: Words superimposed on the picture area, usually in the bottom half of the frame, either as translation of dialogue or to give information about the place, time or action.

SUPERIMPOSITION (super): The placing of one image over another, usually in printing. Thus superimposed titles.

SWISH-PAN see WHIP-PAN

SYNC BENCH see EDITING BENCH

SYNC EFFECTS: Sound effects that are part of the synchronous recording.

SYNC MARK: The mark placed on picture and sound as a level sync reference. Either on the head of a roll or on the individual sync point at each slate.

SYNC PLOP: One frame of tone (usually 1000 cycle) that provides a sync reference opposite a predetermined frame on the leader. Usually placed opposite or in parallel to the '3' on the picture leader.

SYNCHING UP: The process of putting picture and sound material into synchronization.

SYNCHRONIZER: The mechanical device most commonly used for preparing sync material and for conforming the negative or original to the cutting copy or work print.

TAIL, TAIL(S) OUT: The end of a roll of film or the fact that it is wound up end out.

TAKE: The individual attempts to obtain a shot, differentiated by sequential numbering on the clapperboard and the corresponding announcement.

TAKE-UP: Any mechanism on which the film is accumulated after running through a camera, editing machine or projector.

TAPE JOINER (or tape splicer): A device that uses adhesive tape to make the join, usually incorporating a cutting device.

TV CUT-OFF: The area of the frame that is actually visible in television transmission. Important for such things as positioning of titles.

TILT: A shot that uses vertical movement of the camera without changing the horizontal level of the camera body.

TIMING see GRADING

TRACKING: Any shot made by moving the camera and its support, usually on wheels, along a pre-laid track.

TRACKLAYING (or laying tracks): In editing, the process of assembling sound film of all kinds in a form that allows for efficient manipulation during mixing.

TRANSFER: The process of re-recording sound, e.g. from tape to film or film to film. Also the sound thus re-recorded.

TRIAL PRINT *see* ANSWER PRINT

TRIM: A short section of any shot or sound track that has been removed from the take as assembled or cut into the film. Where a shot is used once there will be both a front and end *trim* to be refiled.

TRIM BIN: The device in which trims are hung or clipped *while* the material for a sequence is being cut. It should be cleared constantly during editing and the trims refiled to avoid the problem of not having immediate access to any piece of film.

ULTRASONIC: A method of cleaning dirt from film by the use of high frequency sound waves.

UNDERSHOT: A sequence or a whole film that is inadequately covered in the shooting and thus makes editing unnecessarily difficult.

VIRGIN LOOPS: Mint sound film that is looped for the purposes of recording especially during post-synchronization.

VOICE-OVER *see* NARRATION

WET GATE (or wet printing): Printing that incorporates a small tank of liquid through which the stock passes *before* reaching the point of exposure. *See* LIQUID GATE.

WHIP-PAN (zip-pan or swish-pan): Fast movement of camera during shooting or the shot that is thus produced which blurs the image between two points in a pan.

WILD TRACK: Sound that is recorded in the same situation as any shooting for a film but is not obtained as sync.

WIPE: All optical effects that convey the impression of one shot being removed by the appearance of another. In its simplest form a hard-edged line travels across the screen simultaneously removing the outgoing shot whilst revealing the incoming one.

WORK PRINT: The positive copy of the film that is used by the editor in the process of cutting, from which the CUTTING COPY is produced.

WOW: A disturbance in sound that gives the effect of spasmodic changes in pitch, usually resulting from variations in the speed of the transport mechanism in a recorder.

ZERO FRAME: The first frame of a roll of picture.

ZIP-PAN *see* WHIP-PAN

ZOOM: The act of enlarging or reducing the image in the frame by means of a zoom lens.

Acknowledgments

The author would like to thank Ron Thompson of Technicolor for his comments on Chapter 7, 'The Laboratory in Post-production', Jilda Smith for assistance in the preparation of the Appendix, and Harriet Pacaud for the cover photograph. He also thanks his colleagues for their help and advice, especially Colin Young and Chuck Despins, and Judith McDonnell for typing the manuscript.

Photographs are reproduced by courtesy of the following:
Acmade International, Uxbridge 31, 33, 38; Les Amies de Georges Méliès, Paris 2; BBC Copyright Photograph 15; Contemporary Films, London 6; EMI Films Limited, London 53; Daiei Production 41; Gala Film Distributors Ltd, London 44, 51; Hazeltine Corporation, New York 57; Hemdale Film Group Ltd, London 52; Hungaro Film 46; Kem Electronic Mechanisms Ltd, London for MKM, KEM and Prevost 26, 27, 28; Magnasync/Moviola Corporation, California 22, 23, 24, 29, 30; Molinare, London 58; Mosfilm, Moscow 49; Ernest F. Moy Ltd, London 37; Novosti Press Agency (A.P.N.) 4; Parc Film, Neuilly 43; Photographic Electrical 32; Shochiku Co. Ltd, Tokyo 47; W. Steenbeck & Co. (GmbH & Co.) 25; Toho, Japan 10; United Artists 8, 42, 45, 50.

Film stills were supplied by courtesy of the National Film Archive/Stills Library, London.

Charts are reproduced by courtesy of the following:
Sarah Boston and Omnibus 19; Michael Bradsell and Venom Productions 18, 20; Rodney Holland and the Rank Organization 54.

Bibliography

Barry, Iris, *D. W. Griffith: American Film Master*, New York 1965. Delineates the development of Griffith's use of editing.

Bazin, André, *Qu'est-ce que le cinéma?*, Paris 1958–62, Berkeley and Los Angeles 1967–71.

Bresson, Robert, *Notes on Cinematography*, New York 1977.

Brownlow, Kevin, *The Parade's Gone By*, London and New York 1968. Especially the chapter that includes interviews with veteran editors.

Faure, Elie, *Histoire de l'art*, Paris 1921–7, New York 1921–30. Vol. IV 'L'Art moderne'.

Godard, Jean-Luc, 'Montage mon beau souci', in *Cahiers du Cinéma*, 65, December 1956; translated by Tom Milne, 'Montage my Fine Care', in *Godard on Godard*, London 1972.

Happé, Bernard, *Your Film and the Laboratory*, London 1974. An excellent graphic guide.

Lindgren, Ernest, *The Art of the Film*, London 1948.

Nizhny, Vladimir, *Lessons with Eisenstein*, translated by Ivor Montague and J. Leyda, London 1962.

Reisz, Karel and Millar, Gavin, *The Technique of Film Editing*, London and New York 1953.

Rosenbloom, Ralph, *When the Shooting Stops the Cutting Begins*, New York 1979. Gives the flavour of feature cutting through one man's experience.

Sadoul, Georges, *British Creators of Film Technique*, London 1948.

Truffaut, François, *Hitchcock*, London 1968; first published as *Le Cinéma selon Hitchcock*, Paris 1966.

Walter, Ernest, *The Technique of the Film Cutting Room*, London and New York 1969. Provides a very good insight into the practice of feature film editing.

Index

Figures in italic refer to illustrations